EDUCATION MATTERS

Genera

ADULT

G000096227

ADULT EDUCATION

Michael D. Stephens

CASSELL

Cassell Educational Limited
Villiers House
41/47 Strand
London WC2N 5JE
England

© Cassell Educational Limited 1990

First published 1990

British Library Cataloguing in Publication Data
Stephens, Michael D. (Michael Dawson), *1936–*
Adult education.—(Education matters)
1. Great Britain. Adult education
I. Title II. Series
374'.941

ISBN 0 304 31949 X (hardback)
      0 304 31955 4 (paperback)

Typeset by Input Typesetting Ltd, London

Printed and bound in Great Britain by
Biddles Ltd, Guildford and King's Lynn

CONTENTS

For Helen Fiona Stephens

FOREWORD

Professor E. C. Wragg, Exeter University

During the 1980s a succession of Education Acts changed considerably the nature of schools and their relationships with the outside world. Parents were given more rights and responsibilities, including the opportunity to serve on the governing body of their child's school. The 1988 Education Reform Act in particular, by introducing for the first time a National Curriculum, the testing of children at the ages of 7, 11, 14 and 16, local management, including financial responsibility and the creation of new types of school, was a radical break with the past. Furthermore the disappearance of millions of jobs, along with other changes in our society, led to reforms not only of schools, but also of further and higher education.

In the wake of such rapid and substantial changes it was not just parents and lay people, but also teachers and other professionals working in education, who found themselves struggling to keep up with what these many changes meant and how to get the best out of them. The *Education Matters* series addresses directly the major topics of reform, such as the new curriculum, testing and assessment, the role of parents and the handling of school finances, considering their effects on primary, secondary, further and higher education, and also on the continuing education of adults.

The aim of the series is to present information about the challenges facing education in the remainder of the twentieth century in an authoritative but readable form. The books in the series, therefore, are of particular interest to parents, governors and all those concerned with education, but are written in such a way as to give an overview to students, experienced teachers and other professionals who work in the field.

Each book gives an account of the relevant legislation and background, but, more importantly, stresses practical implications of change with specific examples of what is being or can be done to make reforms work effectively. The authors are not only authorities in their field, but also have direct experience of the matters they write about. That is why the *Education Matters* series makes an important contribution to both debate and practice.

ACKNOWLEDGEMENTS

It is a singular pleasure to record my thanks to the many people who assisted me with the information and ideas used in the following book. Of those I approached nobody was other than most helpful, and such aid was always given with a remarkable grace. I had expected good-natured assistance from old friends, but I am grateful to others whom I had not previously known and who were so pleasant to deal with.

I have not listed everyone who helped me, since often it was a brief encounter or I was asked not to acknowledge their assistance, but the following colleagues were of particular importance: Neil Barnes of BBC Educational Broadcasting Services; Ian Benson, chief education officer of HM Prison Service; David Hardy of PICKUP, and other members of the DES staff at Elizabeth House; Patrick Knox of the Training Agency in Sheffield, and other TA staff in Nottingham; Sheila Innes, chief executive of the Open College; Dr Eric Midwinter, director of the Centre for Policy on Ageing; Ros Morpeth, director of the National Extension College; Sue Pedder, head of unit, the London Open College Federation; Mike Richardson, Pro-Vice-Chancellor (Continuing Education) of the Open University, who read the whole manuscript; John Taylor of the Educational Counselling and Credit Transfer Information Service; and Dr Noel Thompson, chief executive of the National Council for Educational Technology. Any mistakes in the book, and the views expressed, are, of course, my own.

Finally, my thanks to Professor Ted Wragg, the series editor, and the publisher Naomi Roth of Cassell.

ABBREVIATIONS

AIMER	Access to Information on Multicultural Education
ALBSU	Adult Literacy and Basic Skills Unit
ALFA	Access to Learning for Adults
ALRA	Adult Literacy Resource Agency
BBC	British Broadcasting Corporation
CET	Council for Educational Technology
CNAA	Council for National Academic Awards
DES	Department of Education and Science
ECCTIS	Educational Counselling and Credit Transfer Information Service
EHE	Enterprise in Higher Education (initiative)
EMIE	Educational Management Information Exchange
ESCC	Educational Services Consultative Committee
ESOL	English for speakers of other languages
ET	Employment Training (initiative)
FEU	Further Education Unit
IBA	Independent Broadcasting Authority
ITV	Independent Television
LEAs	local education authorities
MIND	National Association for Mental Health
MSC	Manpower Services Commission
NAEGS	National Association of Educational Guidance Services
NCVQ	National Council for Vocational Qualifications
NEC	National Extension College
NERIS	National Educational Resources Information Service
NIACE	National Institute of Adult Continuing Education
OU	Open University

PEVE	post-experience vocational education
PICKUP	Professional, Industrial and Commercial Updating
REPLAN	DES Programme for the Adult Unemployed
SCUTREA	Standing Conference on University Teaching and Research in the Education of Adults
STEP	Special Temporary Employment Programme
TAPs	training access points
TECs	Training and Enterprise Councils
TG	Townswomen's Guild
TTNS	The Times Network Services
TUC	Trades Union Congress
UCACE	Universities Council for Adult and Continuing Education
UDACE	Unit for the Development of Adult Continuing Education
UFC	Universities Funding Council
WEA	Workers' Educational Association
WI	Women's Institute
YMCA	Young Men's Christian Association
YOP	Youth Opportunities Programme
YWCA	Young Women's Christian Association

INTRODUCTION: DEFINING TERMS

One of the great weaknesses of English educational policy-making is either/or-ism. When faced with two or more educational needs the English invariably assume they are alternatives. Whereas more enlightened countries attempt to cover all rewarding areas of education the English have certain types of provision which will be fashionable at a particular point in time, whilst other equally important work will be starved of resources. Adult education is notably afflicted by this English malady. The English have never been as generous in their funding of education as many other states; it has been suggested that they do not like paying for the education of other people's children. And it is childen whom they see as receiving education. Whilst many modern economies regard the education of adults as of increasing importance, and quite likely in the foreseeable future to outdistance national spending on child and adolescent provision, England struggles to agree a full system of schools, further and higher education. At a time when nursery education provision is modest and England has the most exclusive universities system of any developed country it is hardly surprising that adult education, in many areas of which England was a pioneer, is underfunded and ranging in quality from the superb to the inadequate.

The two traditions

Where either/or-ism is most notable is in the division of adult education between what is crudely seen as vocational provision and non-vocational courses and groups. Since the industrial revolution became full-blown in the nineteenth century there has been a shortage of skilled and educated labour which has tempted governments to direct whatever

1

modest national resources they cared to give adult education towards programmes of an instrumental nature (i.e. seeing the education of adults as an instrument of the economy). Since Prime Minister Callaghan's speech at Ruskin College in 1976 which began the so-called 'Great Debate' on education, succeeding administrations have favoured funding instrumental adult education. Alternative forms of non-vocational adult education have seen a rapid decline in government and local government subsidy.

This book will deal with both forms of adult education provision as they are equally important and show many distinctive English features. However, if more space is devoted to, say, the Training Agency than the Educational Centres Association it is because the present government sees its work as being of enough importance to put into it, by English standards, unheard-of resources whilst it has cut its subsidy to the Educational Centres Association by a third to some £6000 p.a. For England's 46.8 million people to favour only vocational adult education at a time of increasingly complex roles for the citizen is inadvisable. Unfortunately the tradition is one of funding, always relatively modestly, either liberal adult education or the training, retraining or updating of those in, or available for, work. The proclaimed obsession of London governments with the economy since 1976 inevitably makes the latter today's fashion.

Adult defined

What is an adult? Within this volume such a student will be over the legal age of 18 years and will have completed his or her initial education (school and, for the privileged few, higher education). The provision for such adults within England is of considerable diversity. For example when looking at the possible grant-aided contribution of universities the Russell Report of 1973 (*Adult Education: A Plan for Development*, 213.1–213.7.3) listed the following:

a) A continuing provision of liberal studies of the traditional kind, characterised by intellectual effort by the students, the guidance of a tutor with firmly based scholarship, and the customary freedom from externally imposed syllabuses and examinations.

b) 'Balancing' studies of an academic character, designed to complement earlier specialisation in education.

c) 'Role education'. By this we mean education of a liberal and academic nature designed to provide a relevant background of knowledge and appropriate intellectual skills for groups whose common element is their role in society. They may be occupational groups from industry or the professions – such as training and personnel officers, doctors, clergy or social workers – or their role may be voluntary, as with magistrates or local councillors.

d) Industrial education, namely courses of a liberal and academic character related to human relationships rather than technical processes, for all levels of industry from management to shop floor.

e) Project work, in which a group of adult students, under the guidance of a university teacher, engages in a process of research or enquiry one of whose objects is to teach the techniques or disciplines involved.

f) Training . . . for those engaged in the education of adults.

g) Development or pioneer work in connection with special problems of adult education or new fields of work. The grant in these instances would act as a 'pump-priming' for a limited period in the expectation that continuing provision would be made by other agencies or under the university's own financial arrangements. Examples would be: courses in new fields for professional or vocational groups, including refresher and post-experience courses giving access to new knowledge or the results of research. The bulk of a university's work under this heading would be excluded since it is well established and can draw on its own sources of finance; but new developments might need initial support in order to establish themselves or to clarify the nature of the need. Work of an informal or pioneer character with disadvantaged sections of the population, including the training or orientation of those working in such fields, especially voluntarily. Provision for adult access to graduation or other qualification at an advanced level.

As the years since 1973 have shown, these broad categories have fragmented into numerous subdivisions of greater or lesser importance. The increasing provision of the universities in the field of the education of adults has been significant, but no more so than that of polytechnics and colleges of higher education. Particularly in the field of updating, whether by short courses or further qualifications, higher education institutions have greatly extended their programmes, financially helped by such government initiatives as PICKUP (Professional, Industrial and Commercial Updating).

The example of one governmental report's view of what universities should provide for adults demonstrates the complexity of provision in England. The substantially larger providers such as the local education authorities or the Training Agency have an equal richness. Even if the English citizen's appetite for education is not generously provided for by government funds its diversity is as great as that found in any other country. The following pages will do less than justice to that fact.

The English case study

The book also restricts itself to England. Scotland, Wales and Northern Ireland have differences of organisation and emphasis, but much of the underlying educational philosophy is shared. To attempt to describe all four adult education systems would mean a much longer book or unavoidable superficiality. The present debate on adult education, and much of the resulting provision, are similar in countries throughout the developed world. England makes a good case study and, where relevant, supplementary material has been used from other countries. England's provision in many areas, for example the work of the Adult Literacy and Basic Skills Unit (ALBSU), is often of world class, but where it is not, for example in industrial training, it is helpful to look briefly at the reputed international pacemakers like Japan.

The education of adults suffers from a bewildering range of titles. The term 'adult education' is often used in England to signify only non-vocational liberal adult education, but in this book the more usual international interpretation is favoured, that is, education covering all provision for adults. Of recent years the British government has tended to use the term 'continuing education', whilst various international organisations have offered recurrent education, lifelong education, and permanent education. Many academics have made their careers out of debating the exact meaning of the various terms, from the singularly ugly andragogy to the dull post-initial education. What has always been apparent is that the simple title of adult education beats all contenders regarding effective communication with the general public and acceptable English.

Social change

The description of adult education has to be recognised as taking place against a century of dramatic and continuing social change which has, and continues to have, unparalleled influence on the style of provision. Life expectancy has increased by approaching 30 years since 1901. As the Director of the Centre for Policy on Ageing, Dr Eric Midwinter, noted in 1982 'Suddenly the education of elderly people in the United Kingdom has become an important issue'.[1] As so often in human affairs, the reasons are straightforward. There is a much higher percentage of over-60-year-olds in the population, with the attendant political clout. Similarly, divorce was rare at the beginning of the century, but now a third of marriages break down. Some two-thirds of married women now have paid employment, again a contrast with 1901. Although England lags behind its main economic rivals in overall educational provision its population is much more extensively educated than in late-Victorian times. This is partly a response to the disappearance of unskilled jobs. The economy's appetite is for ever more highly educated workers.

5

Greater leisure has often seemed less available than official statistics suggest as wives went out to work and, for the middle classes, the age of servants ended, but the average working week has substantially declined in hours since the 1950s. The changes since my childhood in the 1940s have been notable through many seemingly minor improvements. Whatever we may feel about the pollution and other problems which result from most families' possession of a car, such personal transport has given men and women remarkable mobility and easier access to adult education, whether formally organised or non-formal, and perhaps especially informal. My parents first had a telephone in the 1950s, whilst our children use one without a second thought, as something which has always been there like hot water, television, refrigerators and central heating. It is a surprise to realise that the central heating of private homes in England only began to become commonplace in the 1960s. Most of England's citizens are of the chilblain generation. It is in the many small improvements in people's physical well-being since 1945 that social revolution has taken place. My mother spent long hours darning the family's socks whilst we now throw away such items within months of purchase. We are a throw-away society; previous generations were ruled by 'make do and mend'. The deep freeze and refrigerator have undermined the tyranny of daily shopping. All these aids have released more time for almost the whole population. Except for an underclass, an unforgivable characteristic of a society as rich as ours, life for most English citizens is materially, if not spiritually, much better than that of their parents.

Although virtually all workers now receive at least three weeks of paid annual holiday the rise in home ownership (approaching two-thirds of households are owner-occupiers) often means that such time, and other leisure, is used in home-improvement activities or gardening. These, in themselves often forms of adult education, will not be dealt with in this study. So much learning is of a non-formal or informal nature that to discuss it would make the subject of the book unmanageable.

The rise of unemployment in the United Kingdom to a peak of over 3 million in the mid-1980s, in contrast to 292,000 in 1961, reminded the English that the job market could still fluctuate dramatically, and that some parts of England (e.g. the south-east) were much richer than others (e.g. the north) and less prone to such social devastation as that caused by unemployment. High unemployment has indicated once more that the English education system lags far behind the needs of the economy. Those with qualifications have not normally been the ones to lose their jobs. As the Department of Employment White Paper of 1989 (*Employment for the 1990s*) predicts, England is undergoing rapid changes in demography, technology, market opportunities and skill requirements. The implications for vocational adult education are enormous, with members of the Confederation of British Industry proclaiming chronic shortages in skilled and educated employees. As we shall see, the government has taken belated and, many believe, inadequate initiatives to counter an English industrial and commercial tradition of poaching workers instead of training them.

The inadequacy of the English workforce's attitude to education and training has regularly been noted by writers and forecasters. Most seem to agree with Professor Charles Handy's lecture 'The Future of Work – the New Agenda' given to the Royal Society of Arts on 23 February 1987:

> No one will survive, let alone succeed, in the new world of work who cannot communicate and work with others, who cannot think for himself or herself, who cannot demonstrate some competence, some saleable skill if you like, and who cannot push and shove and take initiatives. Of course the best of British have always done these sort of things, but the best was 10 per cent or perhaps 20 per cent. I'm talking about a minimum of 70 per cent.

With the least educated population of any of the major industrial countries, England will have to look to an extensive development of adult education to provide the sort of workforce Handy is talking about. As this book illustrates, a number of initiatives already exist to help meet such education and training needs, but they are too modest, too narrowly focused, and face the greatest of all problems – a culture which is not 'education minded'.

And those policy-makers who have an interest in education are obsessed with the old school-dominated model. As workers, whether white-collar or blue-collar, are now expected to change jobs several times during their lives, and face change even more often during their period with an employer, the era of lifelong education is with us. It is not just doctors or airline pilots who must expect to return for further training and education. Virtually all workers must now see their initial education as just the first stage of a process which will last until the end of their lives. This new tradition is being established painfully in England. As Tim Brighouse wrote when education officer for Oxfordshire:

> The problem with the British system of schooling in any case is that it has its roots steeped in the language of failure in a way unparalleled in other places, such as North America, with students' grades, their credits, their confidence (albeit somewhat misplaced) and their strong embrace of lifelong learning. Even their universities of 20–30,000 undergraduates boast as much as a third of their students over the age of 30.[2]

The well-educated citizen

However, whilst it is possible to convince those who control resources that vocational adult education needs greater emphasis in our national life, non-vocational adult education receives no such favour. The distinction between non-vocational and vocational is often unrealistic as adults may turn up for vocational reasons to take a non-vocational programme whilst others may pursue a supposedly vocational course for non-vocational reasons. Despite this there is a national belief that adult education when labelled 'non-vocational' is less worthy of official subsidy than when it is proclaimed 'vocational'. For both types of programme there is a tradition which says that investment in child education benefits the country, whilst that in adult education is assumed to advantage only the individual. As will be repeated often, England suffers from the massive economic and social problem that it has yet fully to recognise that a country has only one major resource and that is its people. The better educated all the people are the more effective that resource will be.

Well-educated citizens result from high investment and national commitment to all forms of education and training from what has been called the womb to the tomb. The social well-being of a country is even more important than its economic success. Being rich, whilst greatly to be cherished by a state, is not enough. Non-vocational adult education is of singular importance in achieving and sustaining a creative and stable citizenry.

In a paper submitted as evidence to the Russell Committee Professor Harold Wiltshire wrote of the differences between vocational and non-vocational adult education:

In so far as the argument [i.e. that there is no difference between the two] is rational it usually takes the form of an assertation that the vocational/non-vocational distinction cannot in fact be drawn, that there are no 'vocational' or 'non-vocational' subjects since every subject can be used for either purpose, and that there are no easily distinguishable 'vocational' or 'non-vocational' purposes since every student is likely to be motivated in some degree by both at once. This is to assert that if differences are not absolute they do not exist: that since there is an infinite range of shades of green between yellow and blue, yellow and blue must be the same colour. It may well be true that there is no sharp dividing line between 'vocational' and 'non-vocational' subjects (just as it is impossible to say precisely where green ends and blue begins), but it is none the less true that the non-vocational significance of such subjects as dentistry and packaging seems remarkably thin compared with that of history or biology. And it may well be true that students' motives are (like most human motives) usually mixed, but there plainly is a difference between the behaviour and attitudes of the ninety per cent vocationally-motivated student at one end of the continuum and those of the ninety per cent non-vocationally-motivated student at the other.... The student whose motivation is primarily non-vocational is usually older; his needs tend to be related to the

9

crises of adulthood rather than those of adolescence or early manhood; he sees the subject as significant to him as a man or a citizen rather than as an examinee or a functionary; he adopts the role of student voluntarily; he has to face tasks of unlearning as well as those of learning; his attitude to his fellow students tends to be co-operative rather than competitive; he may be older and richer and more experienced than his tutor; and so on. All these differences imply and necessitate different methods of organisation, of class structure and of teaching, and all are specific to non-vocational adult education.[3]

Although in their recent research report for the Further Education Unit (FEU)[4] Harold Marks and Konrad Elsdon have argued against the vocational/non-vocational categories, concluding, 'All colleges find themselves hampered by the administratively wasteful and logically indefensible vocational/non-vocational distinction', I have been persuaded that such divisions are helpful in this study.

One of the most cogent modern writers on liberal education is the former president of Yale University, Dr A. Bartlett Giamatti[5]. In his Freshman Address of August 1981 he stated:

I believe a liberal education is an education in the root meaning of liberal – liber, 'free' – the liberty of the mind free to explore itself, to draw itself out, to connect with other minds and spirits in the quest for truth. Its goal is to train the whole person to be at once intellectually discerning and humanly flexible, tough-minded and openhearted; to be responsive to the new and responsible for values that make us civilized. It is to teach us to meet what is new and different with reasoned judgement and humanity.

It is to be hoped that the spirit of such statements pervades all forms of English adult education. Important new initiatives can, as we shall see, take on a somewhat narrower focus in education and training provision. For example after the government received the *Review of Vocational Qualifications in England and Wales* (HMSO, 1986) which showed that some 300 examining bodies provided 1.75 million awards each year, a National Council for Vocational Qualification (NCVQ) was set up, and had its first meeting in October 1986. The council is to provide a national framework of vocational qualifications in England, Wales and Northern Ireland. Thus it will be deeply influential in the field of English adult education, its first accreditation of selected qualifications having been made in 1987. Its briefing literature stated:

> Changes to the present system of vocational qualifications in this country are needed to provide a better trained workforce, to bridge the unhelpful divide between so-called 'academic' and 'vocational' qualifications; and to improve the status of vocational qualifications. To encourage more and better raining, NCVQ will establish a National Vocational Qualification framework which meets the employment needs of industry, commerce and the professions. The National Council will work closely with employers, trade unions, professional bodies and the providers of education and training to define the competence requirements – skills, knowledge, understanding and ability in application – upon which the qualifications within the framework are to be based.

Such objectives are both laudable and inevitable in our under-educated country, but their interpretation will be of great importance. The five levels of qualification the council favours – basic level, standard level, advanced level, higher level, and professional level(s) – need to be more than skill training in an age which needs self-confident and adaptable workers and citizens. The description of the basic level is reassuring:

> Ability to perform a limited number of work activities within realistic time constraints (under supervision) to match a minimum employment requirement or for training programmes which prepare for employment such as Youth Training Schemes (YTS). Competence should be based upon a foundation of broad-based vocational education and training, with emphasis on core skills, personal effectiveness and planned work experience.

Similarly, at the other vulnerable provision of standard level (where there is always a temptation to go for a simple basic skill training) the NCVQ states that it should be

> Appropriate to many routine jobs and occupations of a predictable character. The minimum standard should ensure a competent performance under both normal and difficult working conditions

11

with minimum guidance and induction: and allow the individual to demonstrate a degree of flexibility in adapting to new situations.

In his letter to the Prime Minister, Lloyd George, when presenting the final report of the Ministry of Reconstruction's Adult Education Committee in 1919, the chairman of the Committee, Arthur L. Smith (Master of Balliol College, Oxford), wrote:

> That the necessary conclusion is that Adult Education must not be regarded as a luxury for a few exceptional persons here and there, nor as a thing which concerns only a short span of early manhood, but that Adult Education is a permanent national necessity, an inseparable aspect of citizenship, and therefore should be both universal and lifelong.

In 1919 British thinking on adult education was as advanced as that of any country in the world. The so-called 1919 Report became deeply influential in places beyond the English-speaking nations. Unfortunately the reality of provision after 1919 rarely matched the report's vision.

In the defining of terms this book attempts to present both that reality and the often more ambitious aspirations of English adult education. Just as the National Council for Vocational Qualification would no longer be satisfied with skills inculcated by rote learning, so the general ethos of education and training has been shot through with the traditions established by such reports as that of 1919. As the world's first professor of adult education, Robert Peers, noted:

> It is with the liberal principles on which our society is based and which are necessary to its survival that adult education must be largely concerned. But these principles exist not merely in theory; they are also expressed in action, in the movements of history, in the shaping of institutions, in attitudes of mind, and in the relations which exist between individuals and groups within and beyond our own boundaries. The key to them lies, not in narrow vocational studies, however necessary they may be and however much they may be made to lead on to larger questions, but in those which concern man as a human being and as a free and

responsible member of the larger society of the nation and the world.[6]

Notes

1 E. Midwinter, *Age is Opportunity: Education and Older People* (Centre for Policy on Ageing, 1982).

2 T. Brighouse, 'Towards Recurrent and Continuing Education – Education Cycles of Failure' in F. Molyneux, G. Low and G. Fowler (eds) *Learning for Life* (Croom Helm, 1988), p. 17.

3 Reprinted in A. Rogers (ed.) *The Spirit and the Form* (Department of Adult Education, University of Nottingham, 1976), pp. 99–117.

4 H. Marks and K. Elsdon, *Adults in the Colleges of Further Education* (Further Education Unit, 1989).

5 A. Bartlett Giamatti, *A Free and Ordered Space* (Norton, 1988).

6 R. Peers, *Adult Education: A Comparative Study*, 3rd edn (Routledge & Kegan Paul, 1972), p. 353.

Chapter 1

THE EDUCATION OF ADULTS UNFOLDS

Historical shaping

We are all imprisoned by the historical experiences of the country in which we live. What we may or may not do is determined by the attitudes and institutions which have developed over the centuries. Adult education provision within England is no exception. The only revolutions of substance are those of the economy, and notably that of the Neolithic and the industrial revolutions. An instinctively conservative humankind endeavours to channel such economic transformations along familiar lines. Change in social and political terms is as slow as people can get away with. The industrial revolution, which first came to full flowering in Britain in the eighteenth and, notably, the nineteenth centuries, has left the world off-balance in social and political terms. As economic change has followed a remarkably long period of technical innovation so adult education has attempted to adapt pre-industrial know-how and accept post-industrial developments where these are inevitable. Like society as a whole, adult education has seen both an expansion of familiar provision over the past 200 years and the development of new subjects and styles of delivery. To the lecture on theology has been added the distance-learning package on technology.

The most renowned book on such changes is Professor Tom Kelly's *A History of Adult Education in Great Britain from the Middle Ages to the Twentieth Century*, first published by the University of Liverpool Press in 1962, with a second edition in 1970. Whilst it is important to note that Kelly explored the Anglo-Saxon origins of adult education, here I shall mainly deal with the nineteenth and twentieth centuries whilst noting the earlier roots.[1]

Nineteenth-century developments

At the beginning of the nineteenth century England's educational provision owed everything to private initiative and nothing to the State. Whilst some key regions of the United States, such as New England, had tax-supported child education from the seventeenth century England had no such tradition to call upon in the full flowering of industrialisation. Child education was provided by religious institutions, by charities, or from private sources. Of the latter perhaps the most notorious were the so-called dame schools. I attended a lineal descendant of such schools briefly in Cornwall in the 1940s. It was run by a middle-aged woman using a house she shared with her sister. All ages of pupils were taken and the teaching was covered by the 'dame'. A weekly fee was charged. The larger schools were given an equally notorious reputation by Dickens, perhaps most famously in chapter 3 of *Nicholas Nickleby*:

> At Mr Wackford Squeer's Academy, Dotheboys Hall, at the delightful village of Dotheboys, near Greta Bridge in Yorkshire, Youth are boarded, clothed, booked, furnished with pocket-money, provided with all necessaries, instructed in all languages living and dead, mathematics, orthography, geometry, astronomy, trigonometry, the use of the globes, algebra, single stick (if required), writing, arithmetic, fortification, and every other branch of classical literature. Terms, twenty guineas per annum. No extras, no vacations, and diet unparalleled.

Working-class education rarely went beyond 8 years of age. In the farming areas children of this age could be employed for simple tasks such as removing stones from the fields, whilst the new factories had an appetite for child labour. For families barely managing to survive the extra income was important.

For many of a population given poor access to education during childhood, adult education became of importance later. The nineteenth century has left numerous records of individual experience such as that of a Cornish miner:

> I was working at Great Cundurrow Mine, which was on the top

of a range of granite hills about a mile from the town [Camborne]. I was working eight hour shifts, and when forenoon shift I should go up a little after 2 p.m. There was no grand dry on the mine then, provided with a bath whereby the men could have a wash before going home. I had to go to the school with my dirty face and hands because I could not stay to go home to wash. At the other shift I had the chance to appear decent. I studied very hard and gained knowledge of arithmetic, mensuration, geometry, algebra, conic sections, and the specific gravities of substance. When I left school I continued my studies at home and commenced the study of trigonometry, land surveying and mine surveying. I did not smoke or drink intoxicants, I put my spare money to buy books, and in a few years I had a decent library. Shortly after this, I commenced the study of theology and joined the Methodist Church. I was asked to have my name put on the plan as a local preacher.[2]

Oliver was remembering the 1840s when 'There were two good schools in Camborne; one was conducted by a man called Chatham, who was a kind of art teacher, that is, he used to teach drawing and beautiful writing. The other man was called John Thomas, and was more of a mathematician and could teach several languages.'

Church provision

The late eighteenth century saw the establishing of Sunday Schools to promote religious education amongst both children and adults. To have access to the Bible, Sunday Schools provided classes in reading. Some went on to develop other subjects. At the beginning of the nineteenth century separate adult schools began to appear, usually dated from the establishing of the Nottingham Adult School in 1798 by the Methodist William Singleton and the Quaker Samuel Fox.

In such provision the Nonconformist churches were most important, none more so than the Methodist church with its strong belief in self-improvement. It developed a highly effective organisation which began with the weekly class-meeting and recruited its class-leaders, local preachers, and ministers from its working-class membership. Later working-class political organisations were to copy the Methodist model. Such successful programmes of adult education left the English with a strong belief in private initiative; the resulting philosophy Samuel Smiles made famous in his 1859 book *Self-help*. Whilst Napoleon's defeat of Prussia at Jena in 1806 convinced many Germans that the well-being of their states depended on having a well-planned and fully government-funded educational system, England put more of its faith into the energies and commitment of the private sector. There is much evidence to suggest that Germany ended up with a more extensively and better educated population, but her critics still ponder the aberration of 1933–45. The belief still lingers in England that somehow the things the state finances are less well done than if private enterprise is employed. Whilst the English suspicion of state intervention may have been good for democracy it has left a malign tradition in education. The often-advocated nineteenth-century belief that government participation in education should be kept to a minimum saw State provision arriving late (the first financial contribution to English education by the State was £20,000 in 1833) and in penny-packets.

Science and technical studies

The need to disseminate widely the new scientific and technical knowledge which the industrial revolution encouraged saw in the 1820s the development of a major adult education movement. The roots of the mechanics' institutes were to be found amongst the workers of Scotland. Mechanics' institutes provided classes in science for artisans and promoted the new culture of the industrial revolution. Whilst many of the institutes initially tried to keep control in the hands of the working-class members virtually all ended up managed by their middle- or upper-class sponsors.

When the London Mechanics' Institute was set up in 1823 it had a library, a museum of machines and models, a public lecture programme, a workshop and laboratory, and elementary classes in arithmetic, geometry, navigation and commercial subjects. In *The History of Adult Education* (1851), J. W.

Hudson recorded that there were returns from 610 mechanics'
institutes in England with 102,050 members. This was not
an exhaustive list, as some institutions did not respond.
Hudson noted 'If the smaller Mutual Improvement Societies,
Christian and Church of England Institutions and Evening
Adult Schools are added to this amount, the aggregate return
for England will be 700 Adult Educational Institutions, with
107,000 members'. Hudson also recorded 'The universal com-
plaint that Mechanics' Institutions are attended by persons
of a higher rank than those for whom they are designed. . .'.
The audiences from the shop floor declined or failed to materi-
alise. Lectures in science were often above the heads of factory workers more in need of literacy and numeracy classes.
Clerks and small shopkeepers were more typical of the audiences of the mechanics' institutes in most areas than the
horny-handed sons of toil the programmes' sponsors had in
mind. Middle-class audiences were drawn in by lectures on
the latest scientific and technical innovations. Itinerant lec-
turers made a handsome income by touring the country
speaking on such topics as galvanism or phrenology. With
such audiences the mechanics' institutes increasingly put on
programmes of a more literary content. English education
has often provided the wrong courses for the wrong students,
whether at mechanics' institutes in the nineteenth century or
through the Manpower Services Commission in the twentieth
century.

A village or small-town mechanics' institute would have a
library, a programme of lectures, and a reading room which
took newspapers, whilst those of the larger towns might provide a secondary school (as at Liverpool) and such facilities
as an art gallery. As Professor Bernard Jennings has noted:

The buildings which were erected to house the institutes – modest
in most villages but often very imposing in the large towns –
formed a useful addition to the social capital of the communities
concerned. The M.I.s had become an established part of the
national life, although within a generation of their foundation
they were generally providing different kinds of education, to

different classes of people, from those envisaged by the founders of the pioneer institutes.[3]

Opinion-leaders within the working class had initially looked to the mechanics' institutes in many towns as a focus for their political aspirations, but they were quickly disillusioned. Such institutions needed the financial backing of the employing classes, and the latter in a period of political unrest were anxious to keep out those they saw as agitators. Most mechanics' institutes were controlled by the middle classes. If a landowner provided a site for a mechanics' institute building he would often state that the institute should not have Chartists as members. There was also a nineteenth-century tradition which discouraged the discussion of political or theological topics within mechanics' institutes. Both subjects were seen as inflammatory.

Technical education in Victorian England illustrated and reinforced still familiar weaknesses in the approach to provision, whether of child education or of adult education. Government was unwilling to provide adequate finance, with the population reinforcing such attitudes by their belief in voluntarism, of which the mechanics' institutes were an example. Factory owners and managers feared the loss of trade secrets if their workmen understood the industrial processes. If the State provided training workshops, they thought the free market would be distorted and government products would undersell their own. As the industrial revolution in its early stages had been the outcome of practical men like Arkwright providing the inventions or improving on traditional practice the country doubted the value of highly educated scientists and engineers. The rule-of-thumb men had made the industrial revolution and so were expected to provide continuing economic success. Too few noted that the second stage of the industrial revolution looked to new products from the laboratory. Those expected to receive technical education were indifferent to it, or found few incentives to persuade them to pursue it. The working class were inadequately prepared by their basic education to be able to follow the technical education courses, whilst the middle classes knew there was status to be gained through a classical education which was not available from any education which dirtied the hands. What was offered in technical education was often too theoretical for workmen and foremen.

Voluntarism

The belief in voluntarism during the nineteenth century saw increasing mutual- and self-improvement initiatives. For example the Rochdale Pioneers Co-operative Society which was founded in the textile manufacturing heartland of Lancashire in 1844 decided that it would grant 2½ per cent of its profits to education. Although not all other co-operative societies followed Rochdale's example, many did. Technological developments saw the cost of printing decline substantially and the establishing of cheap publishing which was promoted through such agencies as Brougham's 1826 Society for the Diffusion of Useful Knowledge. The latter lasted for 20 years to provide cheap educational literature for the working classes, including the *Penny Magazine* and the 'Library of Useful Knowledge'. Whilst many of these innovations met with financial difficulties, they did establish the idea of good, cheap literature.

Mutual improvement societies were to be found in most areas of England by the second half of the century, but they were often short-lived. Working men's colleges, of which that established in London in 1854 was the most famous, were an attempt to broaden out the curriculum offered to the masses. Their origin is usually seen to be the Revd R. S. Bayley's 1842 Sheffield People's College. The college's classes, held at 6.30 a.m. and at 7.30 p.m. for ninepence a week, included grammar, geometry, geography and drawing, but also Greek, Latin, modern languages, literature, logic and history. As Bayley stated, 'among the toiling masses of the town there might be a latent perception of the beautiful, an ardent love of the true'. Unfortunately in 1846 Bayley was expelled from his church, and left for London in 1848. The college continued, but its programme became narrower and more practical.

However, Bayley's belief in providing teaching in the humanities illustrates a continuing theme of English education. Many of those who have promoted mass education have felt that the subjects favoured by the privileged classes should also be available to the working class. Unfortunately the lavish resources available, say, at Eton have not been matched by the State in inner-city comprehensives. Similarly there has often been a feeling that the State must at least subsidise industral and commercial adult education because of the need for better-trained workers, and because economic rivals do, but that 'non-vocational' adult education is less worthy of taxpayers' support. Although the nineteenth century increasingly saw State funding drawn into education, the debate on what should or should not be aided continues unabated today. Current hostility to public spending is no new development, but represents a return to the mainstream of English tradition.

The London Working Men's College was part of the Christian Socialist movement which was founded by Frederick Denison Maurice and his friends in 1848. That was the year of a further French revolution and of the Chartist demonstrations. To bridge the gap between the alienated working classes and the comfortable middle classes Maurice hoped to combine socialism and Christian traditions. The movement had influential supporters. Charles Kingsley's two Christian Socialist novels *Yeast* and *Alton Locke* were widely read, if not always approved of. Evening classes, social work, and co-operative associations were of varying success. Education was seen as the solution to class tensions and social problems. News of the Sheffield People's College led to the foundation of the London Working Men's College in Red Lion Square. It was to be for those aged over 16 who had mastered the three Rs. The curriculum favoured the humanities and was taught by a singularly distinguished band including Ruskin, Rossetti, Burne-Jones, and the author of *Tom Brown's Schooldays*, Thomas Hughes. This was within the tradition of the privileged making available their talents for the teaching of the underprivileged. Previously a number of middle-class literary and philosophical societies' members had given lectures and courses free of charge to their local mechanics' institutes. It was a middle-class version of *noblesse oblige* which has continued as part of the underlying philosophy of English voluntarism.

The Royal Commissions

Although there were a number of Royal Commissions on education during the first decades of Victoria's reign, the continuing inadequacies of the elementary and secondary schooling system encouraged the development of evening schools. The importance of their work was recognised by the first award of government grants in 1851, which were increased in 1855 and 1858. Legislation in 1862 confined grant-aided work to elementary education, and attendances fell. The 1893 Code of the Committee of Council in Education (a mainly liberalising government initiative) led some school boards to provide more advanced instruction. This raised the question of whether grant-aided evening schools were part of the elementary education system, or further and higher education. In 1900 the Cockerton Judgement found against the London School Board which had been using ratepayers' money to teach advanced courses in its evening schools.

The 1861 Newcastle Commission reports had recognised three categories of evening school: those taught by masters of private day schools, those attached to Sunday Schools, and those run by mechanics' institutes. It also confirmed that England suffered a desperate shortage of good teachers, and that evening schools were better suited to providing secondary education but had to concentrate on elementary schooling because of the inadequacy of daytime provision for children.

The 1870 Education Act set up local school boards to fill the gaps in elementary schooling left by voluntary provision. This has been a repeated experience in all areas of English national life. The inability of private initiative to provide a national system is eventually reluctantly recognised by a government when, usually, the crisis is full-blown. Once proper national provision has been established then there continues to be an influential lobby which would like to return to a system of non-government participation. In most instances the members of such a pressure group are already able to pay for expensive alternatives to state provision. Voluntarism has the comfortable middle classes as its ideological heartland.

The 1870 Act did not make elementary education compulsory; that became the law in 1876. Nor did it make it free, which was the case only after 1891. In 1900 many children were still leaving full-time schooling at 12 years of age. To someone coming from a family which is somewhat obsessional about education, it was a shock on marriage to find that my mother-in-law had left school to work in a cotton mill in Chorley in Lancashire at the age of 12. Although such child workers in the 1920s were expected to attend part-time schooling each week, this was not always effective. It is little wonder that so many of the English continue to believe that 'education is not for the likes of me'.

In 1852 the Society of Arts established a union of mechanics' institutes, and in 1856 started to organise examinations. The government's Science and Art department, established in 1853, began augmentation awards to science teachers in 1859, and examinations in science and technical subjects in 1861. By 1880 there were 70 mechanics' institutes running programmes under the Department of Science and Art's examination scheme with some 7,000 students. The Department made a grant to teachers engaged in such courses according to the results achieved by their students. The payment-by-results tradition has continued to seduce various governments, with largely baleful outcomes. It dissuaded many institutions and individual teachers from providing adult education programmes, or led to often narrowly focused and unimaginative provision where the Department of Science and Art certificates were pursued. However, such initiatives by the Department of Science and Art, by releasing extra resources, did encourage more activity in adult education. The major criticism of the work was that it compared unfavourably with the carefully thought out and adequately funded national schemes in Germany, the pacemaker in such matters. Despite such important new initiatives as the Manpower Services Commission (and its successor, the Training Agency) West Germany continues to have a more impressive technical education system than England. Approaching 200 years of government-funded provision in West Germany suggests certain practical advantages over England's *laissez-faire* tradition.

Two Royal Commissions (The Devonshire Report on Scientific Instruction and the Advancement of Science 1872–75, and the Samuelson Report on Technical Instruction 1882–84) and a Select Committee saw the passing of the 1889 Technical Instruction Act which permitted a penny rate to be raised for technical education, and the setting up of technical instruction committees. The following year a tax on whisky (Local Taxation Act) provided funding for the new committees. Under this legislation England's technical education system was substantially founded, with a number of mechanics' institutes absorbed into the local-authority structure. Other mechanics' institutes turned to more leisure-based activities, closed, or were put to alternative uses (for example the Manchester Mechanics' Institute of 1824 eventually became the University of Manchester Institute of Science and Technology).

Public libraries and museums

Two of the tools of adult education were helped by government legislation. The Public Libraries Act of 1850 did not allow the use of ratepayers' money for the purchase of books, but if two-thirds of ratepayers in a special poll agreed, expenditure on buildings and maintenance could be made. The first public library opened under the Act was at Manchester in 1852. An 1855 amendment increased permitted expenditure to a penny rate, and allowed such taxes to be used for the purchase of books and newspapers. By 1869 some 35 authorities had adopted the Act.

At the beginning of the nineteenth century there were few public art galleries or museums, the notable exceptions being

London's National Gallery and the British Museum. The first
40 years of the century saw the development of many
museums, if far fewer art galleries. Prior to the Museums Act
of 1845 there were some 40 museums scattered throughout
England. Most were attached to literary and philosophical
societies or mechanics' institutes or to the specialist societies
which were a feature of the nineteenth century, such as antiquarian or natural history societies. The Penzance Natural
History and Antiquarian Society was typical of such initiatives, and illustrated the weaknesses of the system. The
society had been founded in 1839 but lapsed, to be revived
in 1862. The museum was the society's centrepiece, and was
for the benefit of members and their families, and visitors
introduced by members. Four part-time curators were elected
each year to look after it. The society was allowed to appoint
one or more sub-curators who would be paid for their services,
but the society's finances were rarely healthy enough to fund
such an appointment.

The society's exhibits were largely donated. The *Trans-
actions of the Penzance Natural History and Antiquarian
Society* are full of reports of crises related to the museum,
such as that in the 1880s: 'You are aware the Ornithological
Collection is in a sadly impoverished condition, and it is
impossible to restore it without funds; and the Curators will
inform you that an Entomological Cabinet is urgently needed
(the present one being filled)'. Scores of other nineteenth-
century societies' reports were filled with evidence of
ambitious, by local standards, museum plans never being
matched by resources. Underfunding is not a uniquely English phenomenon, but we seem to underfund more consistently than many other countries.

The Museums Act of 1845 permitted authorities to establish rate-aided museums. Only a few local authorities
initially took advantage of the legislation, in the first five
years of the Act notably Canterbury, Ipswich, Leicester, Sal-
ford, Warrington and Winchester. Until 1880 a majority of
new museums were the result of private enterprise. The Sci-

ence Museum and Victoria and Albert Museum developed from the South Kensington Museum, which opened in 1857.

Notes

1 See also G. W. Roderick and M. D. Stephens, *Education and Industry in the Nineteenth Century* (Longman, 1978) and *Post-School Education in Nineteenth Century America and England* (Croom Helm, 1984).
2 T. Oliver, *Autobiography of a Cornish Miner* (1914), p. 17.
3 B. Jennings, *The Education of Adults in Britain: A Study of Organisation, Finance and Policy*. Newland Papers no. 10 (Department of Adult Education, University of Hull, 1981, 1985, 1989).

Chapter 2

UNIVERSITIES AND ADULT
EDUCATION

England entered the nineteenth century with only two universities: Oxford and Cambridge. By mid-century two more had been added (London and Durham). The second half of the nineteenth century saw the creation of the provincial universities, beginning with Manchester in 1851. After visiting the new University of Durham in 1838 the distinguished American scientist Asa Gray proclaimed, 'I cannot express ... the profound contempt I feel for the English University system of education'.[1] There is little doubt that English universities did not compare well with higher-education provision in nineteenth-century Germany. The establishing of provincial universities in the industrial and commercial cities such as Liverpool, Leeds, Sheffield and Birmingham did much to remedy the too obvious limitations of Oxbridge, such as reluctance to accept new subject areas or to widen the recruitment of students and staff. Throughout the nineteenth century there was widespread discontent with Oxford and Cambridge which was not defused by the 1852–53 Royal Commissions on the universities.

Such discontent partly fuelled the development of university extension. Not only were new universities created, but itinerant university teachers provided lectures in towns and cities throughout England. Although the University of Glasgow had initiated such programmes for its region in the eighteenth century, the modern university extra-mural tradition was established by James Stuart, a Scot, who was a Fellow of Trinity College, Cambridge. In 1867 he had given a series of lectures (in each instance eight) in Leeds, Liverpool, Manchester and Sheffield for mainly female audiences, perhaps half of whom submitted written answers to questions he set.

His subject was the history of science. Stuart's initiatives were to bring to light two major audiences for higher education: middle-class women and working-class men. As critics were fond of saying at the beginning of the century, only Turkey provided as little access to higher education as England.

In 1871 Stuart asked the University of Cambridge to take over the extension work. His plea was supported by the North of England Council for Promoting the Higher Education of Women, the Crewe Mechanics' Institute, the Rochdale Pioneers, and the mayor and citizens of Leeds. Other organisations later added their voice. In 1873 the university agreed to a trial period and that year saw three courses each in the towns of Derby, Leicester and Nottingham. Further programmes in other towns followed in the spring of 1874, and the scheme was then placed on a permanent foundation with Stuart as secretary until 1875 when he was appointed to a chair at Cambridge (professor of mechanism).

London, Oxford and the Victoria University (Manchester, Liverpool and Leeds) established extension lecture programmes in the light of the Cambridge decision. The cost of the lecture courses, which was substantial, had to be met locally, so large audiences were needed. After the lecture a student could attend a discussion group, submit essays, and take an examination at the end of the course. There were also Oxbridge summer schools. The high fees meant that working-class students had to get sponsorship from some local organisation such as a co-operative society.

The impact of university extension, despite the disillusionment over often poor working-class recruitment and the need for short courses to attract enough students to fund the enterprise, was often greater than might have been expected. For example in 1875 an anonymous donor in Nottingham provided £10,000 to support university extension lectures. In response to this generosity the Corporation of Nottingham agreed to erect and maintain a building and to fund instruction. The result was the laying of the foundation stone for the University College building in 1877 and the college's opening in 1881 with professors of literature, physics, chemistry and natural science. The University College's commitment to adult education from such beginnings was considerable. In 1920 it created the country's first department of adult education, and the director of the department, Robert Peers, was made in 1922 the world's first professor of adult education (the second was at Columbia University, New York). Sadly, in the latest version of its University Plan (1989) Nottingham ignores the unusually important national role of the department since 1920 and seeks cuts in its budget of £250,000 (on top of a previous year's cut of £100,000).

Evening schools

The new regulations of 1893 gave more generous grants to evening schools and by 1902 student numbers had increased almost fivefold to over half a million. The 1902 Education Act made county councils the main local education authorities, with wide powers of adult education provision, and the major channel for administering government grants. From this developed the local service role of the 'night schools'. At its best it responded quickly and sensitively to local needs, despite being under-resourced and relying mainly on part-time teachers.

The Workers' Educational Association

The tradition of voluntarism provides great strengths in English national life. My only criticism is that it is used to exclude governmental contribution when only the resources of the taxpayer are adequate for the job. The English have often had a flair for recognising a need and then using voluntarism to attempt to meet it. The beginnings of the Workers' Educational Association (WEA) represent an excellent case study of this. A Gloucester carpenter's son born in 1876, Albert Mansbridge left school at the age of 14, and became a clerk with the co-operative society. His mother introduced him to adult education, and his attendance at university extension and evening classes in London enraptured him. He considered that education should be available to the most humble. In his early writings he sought an alliance of trade unions, co-operative societies and the universities to provide education for a working class to enrich democracy.

In May 1903 Mansbridge and his wife launched an Association to Promote the Higher Education of Working Men. His wife contributed 2s.6d. and appointed Mansbridge honorary secretary. Working-class organisations and universities responded quickly and a first branch was established at Reading in 1904 and branches at Derby, Rochdale and Ilford in early 1905. In 1905 Mansbridge became full-time general secretary on a salary of £50 p.a. with his office in his Ilford home. Within five years there were 5,000 members in 50 branches.

Those local working-class institutions, such as trade unions, interested in adult education made up the membership of most branches. The early branches were often in a community with an established university extension tradition, and Mansbridge and his supporters were keen to build upon that tradition. They approached the University of Oxford to establish a system of tutorial classes for working people (an idea from a London University conference of 1906). In 1907–08 there would be tutorial classes for up to 30 students over two years (quickly extended to three years). Local control of the tutorial classes would be in the hands of the WEA branch. Those who had been members of the tutorial classes could go on to full-time diploma study at Oxford. The government agreed to provide grants for the tutorial classes. By 1913–14 other universities were participating and there were 142 tutorial classes with well over 3,000 students.

The universities paid approaching half the teaching costs of the tutorial classes, and the Board of Education almost a third. For the rest there were grants from the local authorities and from other sympathetic sources such as private charities. In 1913 the Board of Education issued 'Regulations for Tutorial Classes' and undertook to meet half the tutor's fee up to a maximum of £30 per class.

The tutorial class was an English contribution to adult

education which was imitated in some overseas countries, notably in what is now called the Commonwealth. Over three successive years the tutorial class met for 24 two-hour sessions. The group would usually have about 30 students, who were mainly concerned with social and political subjects; there was little interest in gaining certificates. Economics and economic history accounted for half the classes in the early years. It was hoped that a student would submit twelve essays in a year, but those who had left school no later than the age of 14 usually found study and writing less fluent than that number assumed.

Many in the universities were enthusiastic about the work. The participation of the working classes made the universities seem less élitist, but it may have also delayed opening up such institutions to a more broadly recruited student body.

To take the university to the working class of Rochdale or Batley might have meant that the university continued to have a middle-class student body on campus. However, such suggestions as that of Arthur L. Smith in 1910 that tutorial class students should come to Oxford in the summer for further study did make some contribution to modifying class barriers. It was hardly the end of the pernicious class system, but was a gesture towards uniting the world of learning with that of labour.

The First World War inhibited the work of university extension, but not of Mansbridge's WEA. By 1918–19 the association had 219 branches with 557 classes, of which 153 were three-year tutorial classes, and 12,438 students. The war encouraged the participation of women students and the Workers' Educational Association ceased to be a male-dominated movement.

There was opposition to the WEA within the working class. In 1899 Ruskin College had been established in Oxford as a residential institution for working-class students. In 1909 left-wing students at the college broke away from Ruskin and set up a rival Labour College. There was a fear that the WEA, despite its democratic structure, was too easily manipulated by the forces of capitalism. The Labour College moved to London in 1911 where it gained the support of some of the trade unions. In 1916 the South Wales Miners' Federation and the National Union of Railwaymen took over control of the Labour College. By 1918 it had some 5,000 students and a Scottish Labour College was founded in Glasgow. Besides classes, the colleges ran correspondence courses. They taught programmes based on Marxist ideology and were committed to preparing workers for the struggle against capitalism. In contrast the Workers' Educational Association accepted the philosophy of the universities with their belief in impartial truth and the solving of disagreements through debate and discussion. Inevitably the Labour Colleges competed with the WEA for working-class support. Most of the trade unions remained neutral in the dispute. The Labour Colleges organised their ex-students into the Plebs League, which published a monthly journal, *The Plebs*.

The WEA branches offered programmes of tutorial classes, study circles, and shorter courses. In 1924 the Board of Education extended its grants to the WEA to aid shorter courses. Many university programmes were also helped financially. Increasingly WEA courses were taken by paid part-time tutors, rather than unpaid volunteers, and money from such charities as the Carnegie Trust permitted the appointment of full-time organising tutors. The increasing provision of full-time staff, particularly after the Second World War, did lead to subtle changes in the WEA. The professional educationalist often had strong views and the time to try to implement them, whilst the voluntary movement, composed of men and women with other jobs, often found itself with less influence on the Association's direction. This is a tension found in most societies with a tradition of voluntarism. Any agency established by part-time enthusiasts will see power move to the professionals when they are appointed as they have more of that critical commodity, 'time'. Similarly, as the title 'professional' implies, they are usually carefully prepared for the role within the voluntary agency in a way that part-timers may not be.

The WEA has had considerable influence on English national life. Many trade-union officials, councillors and Members of Parliament have been WEA students or tutors. In the 1945 parliament 70 MPs had such a background, and fourteen members of the government. Although the WEA has had relatively small numbers of students – 64,000 in 1937–38 and less than 200,000 today – it has recruited many working-class leaders. Its present 900 branches touch numerous parts of the local communities and include large numbers of local opinion-leaders.

Adult schools and others

In non-vocational adult education the inter-war period saw the establishing of the twin foci of provision of the universities and WEA on the one side and the increasingly effective local education authorities on the other. Other forms of provision were in decline. In 1899 the National Council of Adult School Associations had been founded with 350 schools and 45,000 members. Adult schools were very successful prior to the First World War, peaking in 1909–10 with 1,900 schools and 100,000 members. In 1914 the title National Adult School Union was adopted. In 1917 correspondence courses were added to the adult schools' tradition of lectures, classes, study circles, weekend schools and Sunday bible study. The work of the National Adult School Union continues through its annual *Study Handbook* (first issued in 1911), study groups, summer school, day seminars, weekend schools and foreign study tours, but it is much smaller in its membership.

Quakers were influential in the National Adult School Union, and in establishing ten educational settlements between 1903 and 1918. The first two were residential (Woodbrooke and Fircroft), but the others were not. The common philosophy was grounded in adult education, the promotion of fellowship, and a strong sense of the spiritual. Fircroft College of Residential Adult Education now offers a one-year full-time residential course or a two-year part-time course for working-class men and women in economics, history, literature, mathematics, philosophy, politics and sociology. It is for anyone over 21 years of age and requires no previous qualifications. Woodbrooke seeks to prepare men and women for 'responsible living' through the study of modern religious thought, peace studies, international and social affairs, and Friends' beliefs and practices. The first of the non-residential educational settlements was Swarthmore in Leeds, established in 1909. The educational settlements reminded the English that adult education prospered when it had its own building and a distinctive viewpoint.

In 1921 Albert Mansbridge and Lord Haldane had founded the British Institute of Adult Education, the forerunner of today's National Institute of Adult Continuing Education (NIACE). Mansbridge's creativity was extraordinary. In 1918 he had established the World Association for Adult Education, and in 1919 the Seafarers' Education Service. The latter was committed to providing on-ship libraries for the Merchant Navy and fishing fleets, and to the promotion of seafarers' education through correspondence courses and other programmes. The Marine Society, founded in 1756, has incorporated the Seafarers' Education Service (later Seafarers' Libraries), the College of the Sea, and Ship Adoption. Mansbridge's institution of a first-class library and educational service for seamen continues impressively.

Local authority provision

The British Institute of Adult Education did much to encourage the local authorities in their provision of recreational classes. The evening continuation institutes developed into the evening institutes which, with the technical colleges, provided part-time vocational courses. During the 1920s this work was expanded with the increasing number of national certificates. It was a cheap but wasteful form of industrial and commercial training through adult education. Alongside such vocational provision the evening institutes provided craft and recreational courses. In 1913 the county council in London had established specialist institutions to cater for the demand for non-vocational adult education, but between 1918 and 1939 only a small number of other local education authorities copied the London model. Further impetus to the development of local authority non-vocational adult education was provided by the Board of Education's decision to create an adult education committee under the chairmanship of the president of the WEA, Bishop William Temple, in 1921. The surveys of adult education provision conducted by the British Institute of Adult Education and the Board of Education's adult education committee were both revealing and influential in the making of national and local government policy. London County Council was the model such reports used as an example for other authorities. Other innovations, such as the rural community councils which began in Oxfordshire in 1919, helped to promote adult education provision. The 1933 Adult Education Committee report showed that in 1929–30 the local authorities of England and Wales outside London had organised 11,142 non-vocational adult classes, of which 62 per cent were in practical subjects such as handicrafts, health and domestic courses, 29 per cent in academic subjects covering languages, literature, drama and natural science, and 9 per cent in recreational subjects such as music, physical training and folk dancing. In contrast, of London's 4,886 courses 22 per cent were practical, 33 per cent academic, and 58 per cent recreational. During the inter-war years such provision was hampered by poor accommodation and few facilities. The rapid development of local education authority non-vocational adult education was to come after 1945. The period 1918 to 1939 was often more impressive in its debates about adult education than in its provision. New ideas included Henry Morris's village college plan:

> a system of village colleges which would provide for the co-ordination and development of all forms of education – primary, secondary, further and adult education – together with social and recreational facilities, and at the same time furnish a community centre for the neighbourhood.[2]

Morris saw only four of his planned eleven institutions in Cambridgeshire built prior to the Second World War. His ideas, developed when he was Secretary for Education for

Cambridgeshire, were deeply influential, but more notably after 1945 when greater resources were more available, than in the Depression-stricken 1930s.

Post-1945 developments

The England which emerged from the Second World War had enhanced social expectations. Education was seen both in its traditional role as a gateway to better jobs, and also more clearly as part of the 'good life'. Particularly after the 1950s, rising expectations were built on the 1944 Education Act, which aimed to provide wider access to various forms of education. Between 1958 and 1961 alone seven new universities were founded. A 1966 government White Paper *A Plan for Polytechnics and Other Colleges* saw the establishing of 29 polytechnics in England over the following years. In the 1950s some 4 per cent of the age cohort went to university, whilst by the 1980s approaching 14 per cent were in higher education. Of course this compares very unfavourably with a country like Japan, where 37 per cent of 18-year-olds go on to full-time university courses. In 1969 the Open University was given its Royal Charter, and by 1987 82,000 adults had gained OU degrees.

University departments of adult education after 1945 tended to draw away from their WEA partners, with separate programmes increasingly recruiting those students who already had an above-average level of education. Both the WEA and the university departments of adult education were able to expand their full-time staff numbers through extra funding from the Ministry of Education (formerly the Board of Education). An attempt by the Minister of Education, Florence Horsbrugh, in 1953 to cut government funds to adult education by 10 per cent led to a well-orchestrated public outcry and the resulting establishment of a committee in June of that year under the chairmanship of Dr Eric Ashby,

> to review the present system by which the extra-mural departments of universities, the Workers' Educational Association and the other responsible bodies provide local facilities for adult education, with special reference to the conditions under which the

facilities are organised and are aided by grant from public funds: and to make recommendations..

The 1954 Ashby report, *The Organisation and Finance of Adult Education in England and Wales*, was remarkably sympathetic to the work of the agencies reviewed, and gave further momentum to adult education.

In 1964 the Council for National Academic Awards (CNAA) was granted its Royal Charter to award degrees and similar qualifications for courses to which it had given its approval. Besides extending substantially the number of part-time degree programmes in England, and replacing much of the external provision of the University of London, the CNAA has encouraged many trends beneficial to adult students such as its credit accumulation and transfer scheme (see p. 115), and its association with polytechnics and colleges of higher education with their encouragement of mature-student entry.

During the 1970s there was a substantial cut-back in teacher-training places at colleges of education. Some colleges were closed, whilst others were amalgamated with neighbouring institutions (for example Nottingham College of Education was absorbed by the local polytechnic). There remained 63 colleges which diversified their programmes and took the title of college of higher education or institute of higher education. These added substantially to the higher-education degree courses in England, and many set up programmes of adult education. Institutions like Edge Hill College of Higher Education and Gwent College of Higher Education have appointed directors of adult continuing education.

The substantial changes in English higher education were mirrored, if at times less dramatically, in local education authority adult education. The evening institutes lost much of their pre-war night-school character. With the raising of the school-leaving age to 15 in 1947 and to 16 in 1972, the tradition of the evening continuation school dropped away. There was less need to supplement initial education with night school as the former became of greater length and generally of a better quality, and as more pupils stayed on at school after the age of 16. The evening institutes saw fewer examination courses, and the development of the majority of their provision in the non-vocational sector. Although most evening institutes used school premises there was an awareness of the need for better accommodation and some authorities provided separate facilities. More full-time staff were appointed to look after adult education in the local authorities, although at the end of the 1960s part-time organisers still outnumbered full-time centre heads (1,713 to 842), and there were only 336 full-time teachers of adults as against 76,000 part-time. By the early 1960s the local education authorities had over a million adult students each year in their non-vocational courses.

Professional staff and training

The increase in the number of full-time adult education staff caused a demand for training courses. Although the University of Nottingham had developed a certificate and a diploma in adult education in the 1920s this initiative proved premature. It was the University of Manchester's creation of a diploma in adult education which signalled an increasing interest in training programmes, beginning in the 1950s. For many full-time adult educators the diploma in adult education became the recognised professional qualification. Those who gained such diplomas often then sought a higher degree. As the professional adult educators gained their qualifications so they became more interested in improving the quality of their part-time tutors through training. An *ad hoc* system of part-time tutor training, which ranged from the excellent in some local education authorities to the non-existent in others, was given more cohesion in the later 1970s when the Advisory Council for the Supply and Training of Teachers set up a working party. Its report proposed that all part-time tutors should have the chance to take a stage 1 training course of some 30 or so hours before they taught a local-authority adult class. This would equip them with basic knowledge. A stage 2 course would provide a follow-up with about 120 hours of further information covering topics such as the psychology of adult learning. Both stage 1 and 2 courses would be provided by the local education authority. A post-stage 2 certificate, commonly called a stage 3 certificate, was also proposed for those completing the stage 2 course who wished to study further. The stage 3 certificate was loosely based on the colleges of education (technical) certificate of education. Some universities and higher-education institutions have validated stage 3 certificates. For example the University of Nottingham provided a stage 3 Certificate of Education (Education of Adults) for the Inner London Education Authority and for Lincolnshire.

The development of stage 1 training courses in most local education authorities did much to improve the quality of the part-time teaching force in adult education. As in all areas of the education of adults it was a further indication of the adult student's rising expectations. The ill-prepared adult education meeting was more likely to be met with resentment whether in industrial training or in cookery courses at the local centre.

The technical developments of the twentieth century helped to produce a more critical citizenry. For example the British Broadcasting Corporation was founded in 1926 with a brief to educate and inform the general public. Early in its development broadcasters and educationalists explored the BBC's potential to have a local impact through 'listening groups', often with a tutor to guide the membership. Despite some disappointment, such provision eventually led to the Open University. After the establishment of the Open University in 1969 it was found that broadcasts played a less significant part in the courses than the correspondence material. The BBC, and later the independent broadcasting companies, have proved a key source of the adult's information. Such important contributions as the BBC's 'On the Move' television broadcasts of the mid-1970s have reminded adult educators of the mass media's unique ability to make the general public aware of important educational issues. 'On the Move' placed adult literacy firmly on the national agenda of priority educational provision.

In the 1960s continuing dissatisfaction with Britain's economic performance saw industrial training once more centrestage. The problems were familiar, for example the previously mentioned temptation of firms to head-hunt staff expensively trained by the more enlightened companies. Small, and even medium-sized, firms lacked the resources to fund training. The 1964 Industrial Training Act attempted to solve such difficulties by setting up training boards covering different industries such as the Agricultural Training Board, the Clothing and Allied Products Industry Training Board, the Road Transport Industry Training Board, and the Hotel and Catering Industry Training Board. The boards were funded by a levy on all firms. The concept was simple, namely that those companies who trained staff should get financial assistance from their board. However, implementation proved much more complex. Although industrial training boards were relatively well resourced by the early 1970s there was some dissatisfaction over their impact. This led to the 1973 Employment and Training Act which on 1 January 1974 gave birth to the Manpower Services Commission (now the Training Agency). This most important of adult education initiatives is explored fully in the next chapter. It has inspired other new training developments such as the already mentioned PICKUP launched by the Department of Education and Science and the Welsh Office in May 1982 to encourage short updating courses for adults in employment.

The 1980s proved a time for pointing up differences in adult education. As has been shown, these dissimilarities had a long history, but a government with a clear ideology is bound to favour some forms of adult education more than others. There was little sympathy for allocating taxpayers' money to subsidising what Professor Harold Wiltshire in 1956 termed 'The Great Tradition' of non-vocational adult education committed to humane or liberal studies:

Our society is competitive and our age technological; the greater part of our educational system must meet the needs and reflect the values of that age. Is it not all the more necessary that there should be one small remaining field of education which does not conform or, rather, which conforms to more lasting needs and to older values – a field of education which, in a competitive world, is not competitive, which in an examination-ridden system is not examination directed, which in a society which is sharply stratified both educationally and socially brings together men and women from different social and educational groups? And is it not important that the values and purposes of the great tradition, though developed in another age, should be carried over into this?[3]

Although there continues to be modest subsidy of local education authority and university extra-mural and WEA provision of non-vocational adult education, the Conservative administration's answer to Wiltshire's questions has, since 1979, been substantially a raspberry. The major national resources, often more generous than in the past, have gone to vocational adult education. The assumed needs of the economy are the priority.

Notes

1 Quoted in A. H. Dupree, *Asa Gray 1810–1888* (Harvard University Press, 1959), p. 78.
2 H. Morris, *The Village College* (Cambridge, 1924).
3 H. Wiltshire, 'The Great Tradition in University Adult Education', *Adult Education* (Autumn 1956).

Chapter 3

ORGANISATION

The national structure

The 1944 Education Act, despite much important legislation since (such as the 1988 Education Reform Act), remains the most influential statute for a great deal of modern English adult education. Section 41 of the Act made it

> the duty of every local education authority to secure the provision for their area of adequate facilities for further education, that is to say, (i) Full-time and part-time education for persons over compulsory school age; and (ii) Leisure-time occupation in such organised cultural training and recreative activities as are suited to their requirements, for any persons over compulsory school age who are able and willing to profit by the facilities provided for that purpose.

Section 42 required local education authorities to co-operate with other providers, and section 53 emphasised the need for 'adequate facilities for recreation and social and physical training' to be established in co-operation with voluntary agencies. Again, as so often in English experience, the amount of freedom of interpretation the legislation allowed has meant a range of levels of commitment by local education authorities to adult education.

England's two-tier local government system has county councils covering more numerous district councils. Local government has a statutory obligation to provide school places for those aged 5 to 16 years, but its post-16 education service responsibilities often seem far from mandatory. A government unsympathetic to public expenditure since 1979 has had a substantial impact on local government spending priorities. Inevitably local authorities have had first to cover those areas of educational provision which are mandatory, which has meant that adult education, and particularly non-vocational classes, has sought alternative forms of funding as the local education authority support has declined. The most obvious result has been major increases in student fee levels. A pioneering study, *Changes in Student Participation in Adult Education*,[1] reviewed non-vocational adult education provision in south-east Derbyshire from 1976 to 1981 during which time student fees increased by 240 per cent. The findings confirmed what might have been expected, that is that those with less money (notably housewives, the elderly, and working-class students) stopped coming and their places were taken by the more affluent middle classes. Numbers did not fall, but the social composition of the students changed.

The local authorities are in partnership with central government in the provision of adult education. Although the obvious government ministry involved is the Department of Education and Science, others have become substantial contributors; for example the Department of Employment through the Training Agency which, although separate from the government, is accountable to the Secretary of State for Employment. The public education sector interacts with institutions outside the local authorities and central government such as the universities and the WEA.

The major contributors to the training sector for the economy are industry through its own schemes, and the Training Agency. The enhanced interest in the vocational training of adults has led such institutions as the Open University to develop programmes to meet the expanding market. Important new initiatives have been launched, both by the government and privately. A notable example was the Open College launched by the Secretary of State for Employment in 1986, with its first broadcasts in 1987. Its brochure *The Opening College* made clear that the government looked to employers and potential students for much of its funding. Its potential role was clearly stated by its chairman, Michael Green:

The Open College is the most significant development in vocational education and training for a generation. Its overall objective is to improve the UK's economic performance, using open learning to widen access to skills training. The College will help employers, providing high quality training at an acceptable cost across a range of skills. The College will benefit individuals too, in work or at home. The discovery of the ability to learn something measurable and relevant at your own pace and in your own time, gives a boost to confidence out of all proportion to the effort involved. The College will help people to make the most of their abilities. The College will work with broadcasters, employers, trade unions and education; with providers of training materials in both the public and private sectors; with examining bodies, with the local authorities, with voluntary agencies and with other major providers of training, such as the armed forces and industry bodies.

As the chief executive of the Open College Sheila Innes confirmed, 'The College is unashamedly about the world of work – about employment, about competences and skills, training and retraining'. Channel 4 in March 1987 signed an agreement to provide airtime, and discussions have also been held with the BBC and ITV companies for possible additional broadcasts. The radio and television contribution is in partnership with printed material, audio and video cassettes and practical kits. 'Courses are being designed to fit the needs of employers and individual students with the emphasis on recognising and developing practical skills.' Programmes are intended to range from helping people with poor communication and presentation skills to aiding those wanting national qualifications through examining bodies such as the Business and Technician Education Council or the City and Guilds of London Institute.

Government pump-priming for the Open College, which is an independent company limited by guarantee and registered as a charity, has been of fundamental importance. Over the past 200 years British industry has had a poor record of investing in training and updating. England has lacked the early governmental leadership in such matters which provides a firm and positive tradition. The importance of high investment in training has been instilled into German employers over a long time, and their experience has confirmed the government's belief. In many ways the Open College is dealing with an industrial culture where attitudes towards investment in training are as they were in Germany in the nineteenth century. The English industrialist is far from convinced that high investment in training gives a good return on his money. In Germany and Japan the view is opposite, but it is significant that in both countries strong government leadership educated Japanese and German employers into such attitudes. The Open College will make a significant contribution to vocational adult education, but its first decade will be a tough one as, with other such agencies, it attempts to change the prevailing English industrial culture.

Besides the public education sector and the training sector, there is a long-established private provision of adult education. Jennings includes in this category of provision

> institutions of higher education; further education and secretarial colleges; trainers in information technology and related business studies; language schools; correspondence colleges; vocational (craft) training schools; professional associations with a training role; driving schools, including some specialising in heavy goods vehicle driving; and 'recreational' providers.[2]

Although most providers in this sector seek a profit through the sale of their services, some non-profit-making agencies are included.

A good case study of private provision is that of the Association of British Correspondence Colleges. Its *Broadsheet* lists 178 subjects in which tuition is available ranging from accountancy to yachting theory and including arboriculture, computer programming, dog judging, electro-therapy, fire-manship, freight forwarding, herbal medicine/phytotherapy, massage and allied therapies, Montessori primary teaching, ocean navigation, quality assurance, romantic writing, spectacle lens design, and work study. Many of the courses are directed at professional and national examinations such as the General Certificate of Secondary Education, or those of the Institute of Chartered Secretaries and Administrators or the Law Society. Nineteen colleges, ranging from the Pitman Tutorial College to the Canine Studies Institute, are members of the association and comply with its code of ethics.

Correspondence education developed during the nineteenth century when the creation of the railways and modern postal system provided the technical developments to sustain it. Statistics on correspondence education have always been difficult to obtain, but at any time in England the number of students using its various forms is probably in the hundreds of thousands. As it is a flexible type of provision where the student has greater control over time, it has been seen as a convenient way of pursuing adult education. However, the relative isolation of those using this style of study has been a major factor in the high drop-out rate amongst students.

The creation of the Association of British Correspondence Colleges in the late 1950s resulted from the uneven reputation of the distance-education courses some correspondence companies offered. Those with good programmes wished to disassociate themselves from providers of poor-quality education. In 1969, after discussion between the Department of Education and Science and the industry, the Council for the Accreditation of Correspondence Colleges was set up with responsibility for establishing national standards of tuition carried out by post. In granting accreditation to a college the council appoints a team to investigate and assess the institution. Such accreditation is normally reviewed every five years. The council also seeks to widen the use of correspondence education.

There is also a massive and ill-defined voluntary sector of adult education which includes such well known organisations as the Townswomen's Guild (TG) and Women's Institute (WI), much of the work of the churches in this area (for example there is a Christian Association for Adult Continuing Education), the Co-operative Educational Association, the Field Studies Council which was created in 1943, the National Federation of Community Organisations, the National Council for Voluntary Organisations, the National

Federation of Voluntary Literacy Schemes, the Pre-Retirement Association, the Pre-School Playgroups Association, the YMCA and the YWCA. The Young Women's Christian Association, for example, provides courses for the unemployed to improve their self-confidence and awareness of other educational opportunities, and programmes for older women to 'widen their horizons', or, through their 'Women at Work' courses, develop their potential.

The above listing hardly begins to do justice to what is a diffuse and ever-changing part of adult education which touches millions of people in any year. The National Federation of Women's Institutes has over a third of a million members, for example, whilst the National Union of Townswomen's Guilds is nearly as large. Both promote education amongst their 630,000 members. The National Federation of Women's Institutes owns a residential college at Marcham in Oxfordshire (Denman College) which runs 300 courses a year. Women's Institutes and Townswomen's Guilds often have strong links with their local education authorities, university extra-mural departments, and WEA districts and branches. Whilst the WIs have a strong presence in handicraft, drama, music and social education, the TGs have been keen on promoting the woman's viewpoint in current affairs.

English adult education is of huge diversity, and no book can do justice to its complexity. Like all systems of education it has its strengths and weaknesses. The richness of the provision is undermined by the frequent inadequacy of resources and the indifference of government and many key citizens to its importance to national well-being. Despite the 1919 Report, one of the great documents in the history of education, the vision and enthusiasm of the adult educator in England is often met by the indifference of the English to matters educational. The banal English style surrounding the 1988 Education Reform Act is in contrast to Japan's National Council on Educational Reform final report of 7 August 1987:

> The forthcoming age will call for a re-examination of human
> civilisation and of the way of life of human beings, and will keenly

47

require the further flowering of diverse cultures and the recovery of humanity. Education has a great mission and social responsibility in helping us meet these demands of the times. Being fully conscious of this mission, those who are concerned with educational reform must restore mutual trust among the different parties in the education sector for the sake of the future of Japan, as well as for the sake of mankind tomorrow. They must thus create fresh vitality and creativity in the world of education.

In Japan education is a serious business. The 1987 Final Report is a controversial document, but no Japanese government would dare to shelve it in the tradition of Westminster.

Notes

1 J. Daines, B. Elsey and M. Gibbs, *Changes in Student Participation in Adult Education* (Department of Adult Education, University of Nottingham, 1982).
2 B. Jennings, *The Education of Adults in Britain: A Study of Organisation, Finance and Policy* (Department of Adult and Continuing Education, University of Hull, 1985 edn), p. 106.

Chapter 4

THE TRAINING AGENCY

All the developed world has woken up to the need for better-educated and trained workers. Practical considerations have brought the adult educators' dream of lifelong education into existence. Modern industry and commerce have an insatiable appetite for skilled and educated workers, and those who have been trained and educated quickly find that their skills, whether intellectual or manual, need updating. It is not just that technology is changing at increased speed, but that society is becoming more complex. A social worker, for example, is as much in need of continuous updating in skills and knowledge as any technologist with British Petroleum.

The establishing of the Manpower Services Commission in 1974 was a symbol of such developments. Any discussion of contemporary English adult education case studies should begin with the Training Agency, to use its present name, because of this symbolism.

Following the government's White Paper of December 1988 *Employment for the 1990s*, in July 1989 the Secretary of State for Employment issued a strategic guide entitled *Training and Enterprise: Priorities for Action 1990/91*. The White Paper provides its inspiration. It is a key document for anyone wishing to understand the direction of English vocational adult education. The principles on which the Department of Employment's approach to vocational adult education are based are similar to those found in other developed countries:

Training and vocational education, including management training and counselling for small firms, must be designed to contribute to business success and economic growth. Employers and individuals need to accept a greater share of responsibility for training, and its costs, while Government has a role in setting a framework

49

and in funding the training of unemployed people. There must be recognised standards of competence, relevant to employment, drawn up by industry-led organisations covering every sector and every occupational group, and validated nationally. Responsibility for delivery of training and enterprise must, as far as possible, be devolved to local areas where people work and are trained. It is there that we need to bring together private and public investment to meet the skill needs of business and individuals. The training must provide young people with the opportunity to secure qualifications based on these recognised standards. Enterprises, individuals and local communities must be able to shape arrangements, programmes and opportunities to their changing needs and circumstances.

This document is the result of harsh experience, and shows awareness of other countries' greater success in producing a culture sympathetic to education and training:

International competition is a major and growing challenge. Our main international competitors put greater priority into ensuring that a high proportion of the population is trained to a high standard. Their businesses put strong emphasis on continuing education and training through life to enable commercial needs to be met. The breadth and depth of their training standards are generally impressive. They treat training as an investment. Our best companies compare well, but for British business as a whole to compete and grow in the post-1992 [i.e. the single European Market] world the best must become the norm.

Whilst the government sees itself as carrying much responsibility for training the unemployed, and notably the long-term out of work, and intends to use the National Training Task Force (see p. 53) to encourage training in employment, 'the main responsibility for ensuring that the training effort in employment is comprehensive, properly focused, and effectively carried out, rests with employers and individuals'. On lifelong education it is noted that

The world in which initial training lasted a lifetime is gone forever. Successful companies increasingly understand this, and increasingly devise arrangements to ensure that they keep abreast of developing skills needs; keep the potential, aspirations and training and development needs of each of their employees under review; and update the skills and develop their employees throughout their working lives. They recognise increasingly the scale of investment an employee represents and the competitive advantage of ensuring that investment grows. Over the coming years we need to develop, particularly amongst employers, a much wider commitment and a much more systematic approach to the continuing training and development of people at work.

To give local focus the government is establishing training and enterprise councils (TECs) which will 'deliver particular objectives and targets relating to Employment Department Training Agency programmes and activities'. It is expected that the TECs will be able to define the vocational adult education needs locally and the efforts that are being made to meet them. The Training Agency has created business growth training as part of the programme to stimulate more industrial education and training. For the unemployed there is the Employment Training (ET) initiative, and TECs will pose such questions as 'How effectively are ET and other measures coping? How, within the parameters set by government, can ET be developed to make local provision more effective?' The Training Agency has recognised the obvious stumbling blocks in English vocational adult education, such as the relative indifference of employers to investment in training, the distinctive needs in each area of the country, the disappointing overall level of education and training in the population, and the tendency of businesses to see the unemployed as a social problem rather than a potential source of labour to train.

The Training Agency expects the skills most likely to be in demand in the 1990s to be in management, and in a wide range of professions such as engineering, science and technology; the skills of technicians operating at National Council for Vocational Qualifications level 4 in science-based occupations and professional services, notably multi-skilled craft-level employees, and enhanced general competence at all job levels. This view coincides with that of other developed countries. The agency defines general competence as covering

51

communication, numeracy, diagnostic skills, business and technological awareness. As change in England is unavoidable the hope is for an adaptable workforce.

The British labour force is expected to increase by a million between 1988 and the year 2000, with 90 per cent of this accounted for by women. Between 1988 and 1994 the decline in the birth-rate means that the number of 16 to 19-year-olds in the labour force will decrease by over 20 per cent. An increasing number of this age-group is also thought likely to remain in full-time education after the age of 16. The smaller numbers of school-leavers entering the labour market will make more important the education and training of older workers to improve their effectiveness. As sources of labour, the long-term unemployed, women returners, ethnic minorities, people with disabilities, and older workers will be of greater significance.

The training and enterprise councils, as described in the Training Agency's 1989 *Guide to the Development of TECs* and *Training and Enterprise Councils: A Prospectus for the 1990s*, are to be independent companies operating under a performance contract. Two-thirds of the board of directors will be private-sector employers of chief-executive or managing-director status. The rest of a council's board will come from education, or trade unions, or the voluntary sector, or public service. The aim is to have some 80 TECs covering England and Wales serviced by 5,000 staff and with approaching £3 billion of public money available. Besides taking responsibility for existing programmes like Employment Training,

The TEC will be a catalyst for change within its community. It will serve as a forum for local leaders to assess economic and social needs, to set priorities for action and to direct resources accordingly. It will develop new projects and activities to increase the effectiveness of training and enterprise markets. It will work with schools and colleges to raise skill levels and to smooth the transition from education to work. And it will play a vital role in promoting the importance of training as a business strategy – as a serious investment rather than as a discretionary cost.

Each TEC will have to produce a business plan for its community which

> sets strategic objectives; describes the economic and social characteristics of the area in the context of national and international skill trends; identifies priorities for training and enterprise in terms of sector, level and location of service; sets objectives for promoting equal opportunities and the health and safety of trainees; sets out an agenda of new activities which the TEC will undertake; and describes the organisation needed to carry out its objectives.

The plan for a TEC will be for three years in the first instance, and then on a rolling three-year basis. Although such plans are submitted to the chairman of the National Training Task Force, the Secretary of State takes the final decision on the plan's approval.

A TEC will have some £20 million annually to purchase management training programmes. Of course there are already similar national contractors for the Employment Training scheme. There will be £250,000 for a TEC's local initiative fund to aid its objectives. A TEC will be eligible for peformance bonuses, and initially the government will match (up to £125,000 per TEC) pound for pound money raised from other sources. A TEC which underperforms consistently will have its contract cancelled. To aid in the formation and development of TECs in January 1989 the National Training Task Force was created, amongst other things to advise the Secretary of State for Employment.

The training and enterprise councils are a logical next step in the developments which began with the creation of the Manpower Services Commission (MSC) in 1974. In 1977 the MSC had published its priorities. It aimed to help to raise employment and reduce unemployment; assist in the development of manpower resources; make a contribution to economic well-being; help those in employment to lead a satisfying working life; improve the quality of decisions affecting manpower; and improve the effectiveness and efficiency of the Manpower Services Commission itself.

A number of early MSC schemes aimed at relieving unemployment amongst the two most vulnerable groups – early school-leavers and those over 50 – were largely unsuccessful, but a report of May 1977 identified the vocational preparation of young workers as a priority concern. There followed the Youth Opportunities Programme (YOP) to 'prepare young people for work and different kinds of work experience'. YOP was aimed at 16 to 18-year-olds, whilst the older adults were to be accommodated by the Special Temporary Employment Programme (STEP). The YOP programme included two-week employment induction courses, and three-month short training courses, or work experience (six months on employers' premises to a year in community service or training workshops). The MSC's original structure of an employment services division and a training division was soon joined by a special programmes division to take care of such initiatives as YOP.

Both Labour and, since 1979, Conservative administrations have been convinced that British industry is not interested in training. Many companies did nothing to train their workers, or if they did send them on courses they were only too happy to leave to the providers such central matters as programme content and duration. Colleges offered traditional fare, which was too rarely updated. The TECs are intended to change this. The Office of Population Censuses and Surveys in its *Labour Force Survey 1983–4* (1986) found that only 40 per cent of the British workforce held qualifications relevant to their occupation.

In 1981 the MSC issued its consultative document *A New Training Initiative* aimed at encouraging those under 18 to stay in full-time education (in Japan virtually all 18-year-olds are in full-time schooling) or enter training; to develop occupational training of agreed standard and with obvious lines of progression; and to open up greater training opportunities for adults. In the same year came the DES/Department of Employment White Paper *A New Training Initiative: An Agenda for Action*, which was to provide one year's training for those leaving school at 16 without a job; various incentives to encourage employers to develop training; the creation of an Open Tech to provide distance learning materials; the replacement of traditional apprenticeships by established standards of craft and technician training; more preparation for work in schools; and better local and national organisation of training. Traditional forms of training like apprenticeships and formal examinations were to be less favoured than the testing of skills competency.

In 1985 the MSC changed its training programmes for those over 18. To help people out of work to gain employment the Wider Opportunities Training Programme was created, which was notable for greater flexibility of approach and the targeting of audiences such as women wanting to return to work. The Job Training Programme was meant to encourage business and management skills. The New Job Training Scheme followed, directed at 18 to 25-year-olds who were offered a six-month workplace training entitlement. All these programmes were beset by some difficulties, for example cost-effectiveness. The Open Tech established in 1982 proved costly and slow in creating distance-learning packages and was later subsumed into the MSC's Open Learning Unit. Distance learning has been sold as a cheaper and simpler alternative to other forms of education, but this is often not the case. Key associated investments, such as training staff to work with distance-education material, have often been neglected.

The MSC's adult training schemes had some 80,000 trainees in 1983–84 and 390,000 in 1986–87. Significantly over 65 per cent of the training was done outside the established education system. Each year one in thirty of the working population was found to participate in an updating course. When the European Single Market comes into being in 1992 the government intends to have trebled this figure.

In 1983 the MSC absorbed Skillcentres into its Skills Training Agency. By 1987 there were 60 such centres for adult training. In 1985 seventeen 'Access Centres' came into being to promote areas of new technology within industry. A mobile training service was also founded. Although the numbers involved in such initiatives were not vast (perhaps 49,000 by 1987) the MSC learned much from them.

In February 1988 the government published the White Paper *Training for Employment*. In particular the document recognised that many of the long-term unemployed lacked relevant skills and education, and were often out of touch with the job market and had poor motivation. The White Paper aimed to re-establish contact with each unemployed worker, improve the information available to them, offer training programmes, advice and other assistance. The Employment Training (ET) scheme which resulted has an annual budget of £1.5 billion and aims to provide up to a year's training for 600,000 people annually. Priority is given to 18 to 24-year-olds, and those between 18 and 50 who have been out of work for over two years, but people over 50 are not excluded. First referral is to a training agent, from whom the participant receives guidance and assessment for two to three days when a training plan is prepared. He or she is then placed with a training manager who is responsible for the programme, which must spend at least 40 per cent of its time on directed training. Up to twelve weeks may be spent on an extended introduction to develop confidence and may include tuition in basic education, computer literacy, communication skills, English as a second language, basic vocational training, counselling, and job tasters. The training plan covers development of personal effectiveness and motivation training as well as occupational skills. Where possible participants follow programmes leading to external qualifications. Those on the course are given a training premium on top of their weekly benefit and also out-of-pocket expenses, such as for travel. Training agents are paid for each trainee placed with a training manager. The latter is paid for each trainee registered, and a weekly training grant. The weekly grant is greater for those trainees with special needs.

In an interview in 1989 David Hardy, the national manager of the DES's PICKUP scheme, stated,

International comparisons in education in general are notoriously difficult, and in continuing professional development (CPD) it is not easy because we are not necessarily comparing like with like. If we take Japan and the USA, the concept of continuing education is so embedded in the culture that they are way beyond what we are likely to be able to attain in the immediate future. We have also looked closely at the West German system. Of particular interest is that, during the recession, German companies increased the amount spent on training, whilst in the UK they spent less.

However, with a culture largely indifferent to the sort of provision the Training Agency promotes, the latter has developed a number of imaginative projects to raise the profile of adult education and make it more accessible. A good example is its Training Access Points (TAP) which provides local information on work-related education and training opportunities. There are computer-backed TAP information points in job centres, libraries and similar central locations, plus mobile TAPs which can visit factories or other workplaces. TAP has commissioned special computer software which permits a search of local learning opportunities and the taking away of any (printed) details the would-be student has an interest in. TAP uses British Telecom's PRESTEL network to dial into such national databases as ECCTIS (see pp. 113–5). TAP has funded an impressive programme of computer research and development in fields such as Smart Database Searcher (software able to interrogate several different databases) and Computer Assisted Guidance to help employers and individuals to determine their needs.

Research carried out for the Training Agency (*Funding Study Research Programme: Some Early Findings*, 1988) for 1986–87 showed that employers reported that just under half their workers had received training that year (on average 14.5 days per employee receiving training). Provision favoured the young, those with qualifications, and the more senior. One in five firms did not train at all during the year. About a third of workers said they had never received any training. Of the £15 billion spent on training some 75 per cent was made up of the labour costs of the trainees and trainers. One fifth of the training was provided by external agencies. Training decisions were found to be based on business imperatives and often on short-term requirements. Only a third of employers who offer training have any plan for the activity, and some 10 per cent undertake formal training needs analysis. A mere 3 per cent of employers who train compare the benefits of the training with the costs incurred. Of the employers who trained 36 per cent had suffered skill shortages over the past year, whilst firms facing international competition tended to train more than others. Over a third of employers who trained gave legislation (e.g. the Health and Safety Acts) as one of the main reasons for training. The incentives for training amongst employees were improved pay, better job prospects, and job satisfaction. The obstacles were lack of time, lack of money for fees and income support, and fear of loss of job security.

Of course certain groups within the English workforce have a long and substantial tradition of vocational adult education. Since 1945 schoolteachers have not only extended their period of initial training, but have seen a rapid increase in inservice education provision. Doctors have had to take updating training seriously, as their field has seen an explosion of new information, techniques and drugs. The major problem for English vocational adult education, as the evidence above confirms, is to spread such attitudes to employers and employees in other areas of national life.

The Training Agency has begun to change attitudes after a period since its inception in 1974 of experiment and often painful learning. Its clearer targeting can usefully be illustrated by two examples. In the Autumn 1988 edition of the *Skills Bulletin* there was a short report on its standards programme. Obviously the setting up of the National Council for Vocational Qualifications is a key element in this area, but the programme is much broader than the NCVQ's brief. The report stated:

Economic performance and individual job satisfaction depend on raising skill levels by getting in place standards of competence across the range of employment. By such standards is meant the competence which people need (by way of skill, knowledge and understanding) to acquire and apply in order to do jobs effectively. The Training Commission through its Standards Programme provides encouragement, guidance and assistance to industry and commerce to develop and implement standards of competence. The aim of the Standards Programmes is to ensure that wherever possible all levels of occupations are covered by employment-led standards ... the commitment and representation of employers coming together in lead industry bodies – such as in the statutory and non-statutory industry training bodies – is crucial to developing standards recognised and 'owned' generally by employers across industries and occupations. It is through such lead industry bodies that the Training Commission is able to channel both advice and financial assistance to employers to develop and implement standards, having first analysed jobs and skill needs.

In December 1987 the Enterprise in Higher Education (EHE) initiative was launched with its main aim 'to assist institutions of higher education develop enterprising graduates in partnership with employers'. Bids were invited for a sum of up to £1 million spread over five years. In July 1988 eleven higher-education institutions were selected to take part in the first stage of the initiative (four universities, six polytechnics and an institute of technology). In January 1989 the Training Agency published *Enterprise in Higher Education: Key Features of the Enterprise in Higher Education Proposals 1988–89*, which summarises the submissions of the eleven institutions and provides much comment and background on the scheme.

These examples illustrate the range of the Training Agency's interests, and its ability to focus on key areas of weakness in the provision of vocational adult education. Its *Corporate Plan 1987–1991* (November 1987) demonstrates its intentions of contributing to everything from literacy and numeracy provision to postgraduate work. Its growing confidence and expertise permit it to comment fruitfully on areas previously the preserve of established institutions such as universities or colleges of further education. For example in May 1989 it published *High Technology National Training*, briefing would-be students on advanced manufacturing technology, artificial intelligence and expert systems, computer and information technology, electronic and microelectronic engineering, biotechnology and new techniques in construction; and in the same year it produced *Improving Quality in Further Education: A Guide for Teachers in Course Teams* by John Miller and Alison Dower. In its most recent annual report, for 1987–88, the Training Commission points out that its adult training programmes dealt with 514,900 people. It is to be expected that this figure will increase as the Training Agency more effectively harnesses new approaches such as its increasing use of open learning (for example *The Open Learning Business* (1989)).

Chapter 5

OPEN LEARNING: THE NATIONAL EXTENSION COLLEGE, THE OPEN UNIVERSITY, THE OPEN COLLEGE AND OTHERS

As editor of *Open Learning in Transition* Nigel Paine states:

> We prefer to define open learning as both a process which focuses on access to educational opportunities and a philosophy which makes learning more client and student centred. It is learning which allows the learner to choose *how* to learn, *when* to learn, *where* to learn and *what* to learn as far as possible within the resource constraints of any education and training provision.[1]

The book was put together as part of the National Extension College's 25th anniversary celebrations. In his essay on 'Delivery and new technology', Professor Tony Bates of the Open University reminds us that

> In the last 15 years we have seen the large-scale and effective introduction of open-learning and distance teaching methods, initially at the higher education level, but now rapidly spreadng to vocational training. During the same period, we have seen a rapid increase in the technologies available to educators and trainers. Face-to-face tuition and textbooks have until recently been the main media used for education and training, supplemented by broadcast television and radio. In the last few years, though, to these more 'traditional' media have been added audio-cassettes, video-cassettes, cable TV, satellite TV, pre-programmed computer-based learning, computer-based communications (electronic mail, computer conferencing, access to remote databases) and interactive video-discs. We are seeing increasing use of these technologies

in open and distance learning, although they can be used to supplement more traditional face-to-face teaching as well. (p. 364).

In 1963 Michael Young and Brian Jackson founded the National Extension College (NEC) to promote 'a major transformation of adult learning in the UK'.[2] It saw itself recruiting from those adults who had got less than they wanted from their initial education, and also those who could not make use of existing facilities. From the beginning distance education was favoured by the college. Janet Jenkins and Hilary Perraton's International Extension College broadsheet on distance learning, *The Invisible College: N.E.C. 1963–1979* (1980), explained why the National Extension College favoured, for example, the use of broadcasting:

> NEC started with a number of assumptions, which have turned out to be broadly true. First, broadcasting makes economic sense; if you want to teach more people you can do so with fewer teachers using broadcasts, and if you reach enough people the cost per student starts declining. . . . Linked to this was the social argument that broadcasting would make it possible for teaching resources to be spread more widely and more equitably than would be possble through traditional, face-to-face teaching. NEC assumed rightly, that broadcasting would bring it more students; for broadcasts bring education out into the open, and in particular give a new appeal and glamour to correspondence teaching. It also hoped that broadcasts would attract students who would not otherwise take up study. Third, there were assumptions about education. The college started out with the belief that 'a combination of means of education will be superior to any one on its own'. Part of the argument here is uncontroversial; often some parts of a course can be taught more effectively in radio or television than in print. . . . Further than this, NEC guessed that students would work harder on courses with a broadcast component than if they were working by correspondence alone. (pp. 63–4).

With the early acquisition of the University Correspondence College and its 3,000 students, the NEC was in danger of becoming just another correspondence college with a range of GCE O- and A-level courses. The decision to set up the Open University with no apparent role for the NEC also put its purpose in question. The NEC's involvement in 'Gateway' courses for intending Open University students postponed answering this question in 1970. The OU's withdrawal of support for the Gateway courses led to a loss of income which was further emphasised by an eight-week postal strike in 1971. NEC crisis years were from 1972 to 1976 when it had all the characteristics of a conventional, if high-quality, correspondence college. It had 5,748 students in 1972 and 7,869 in 1976. NEC decided to move firmly into the State system, whilst not being part of it. What it had to recognise was that it lacked the resources for the sort of back-up the Open University, say, could afford to provide for its students. The NEC developed 'FlexiStudy'. As Richard Freeman stated

> NEC had looked at what makes for a successful distance learnng course and had identified the ingredients, amongst others, as: Distance learning materials; Distance tutoring; Counselling; Face-to-face tutorials; Facilities for practical work (e.g. laboratories, computers); Examination facilities; Library facilities; Access to multi-media resources. What was significant about this list was that, apart from the first item (Distance learning materials) a local college was better placed to provide all the resources than was NEC. Why then did correspondence colleges exist at all? This analysis led to the concept of FlexiStudy which was jointly worked out by NEC and Barnet College of Further Education. In Flexi-Study, the student enrols on a distance learning course with the local college (they may only live 100 yards from it). That college provides: A distance learning text for his/her chosen subject and objectives; a tutor to mark and comment on his/her written assignments; Face-to-face tutorials; Access to labs, computers etc; Examination facilities; Counselling. Students can then study at home, posting off assignments to the college just as if they were NEC or Open University students. The local college becomes a local distance learning college.

Of course, the NEC was the local college's source of distance-learning materials. With relatively few students for a particular course it is not economic for a college of further education to prepare such material, whilst the NEC, which serves hundreds of colleges, can afford to write, edit, design and print the learning texts. The scheme was piloted in 1977, and by 1983 FlexiStudy was operating in 130 colleges with some 10,000 students. The NEC now has over 200 colleges registered as FlexiStudy centres. Perhaps a weakness in the concept is the varying quality of the colleges' input.

Distance education means instruction which is not face to face. Open learning implies greater access to education for more people. Distance education and open learning are often in association, but this is not inevitably so. However, an institution like the NEC aimed at promoting both. Like the Training Agency it has often acquired its knowledge of such educational provision through harsh experience. For example in 1964 its history of technology course broadcast late on Thursday evenings, 'Towards 2000', enrolled just six students, and in 1978 'World Powers in the Twentieth Century' was an equal failure at recruitment. But the NEC has found that there is a good demand for formal subjects at a lower level. For the first run, for example, of the basic numeracy course, 'Make it Count', using television and printed materials, the NEC sold 5,000 copies of the workbook. As Jenkins and Perraton note, 'It would seem that when a course is directed at a clear need of a particular group, broadcasts can pull in a high proportion of that group'.[3]

By 1988 the NEC had enrolled over a quarter of a million students during the 25 years of its existence. Ros Morpeth, director of the National Extension College, writing about 'The National Extension College: Looking to the Future' noted the diversification of the NEC's activities since the 1960s, but stated:

The new areas of work have important features in common: they all build on NEC's experience in developing open-learning materials and systems and provide other organisations with the resources they need to run their own schemes. These resources include: the development and production of open-learning materials; consultancy for industrial clients; support for the Flexi-Study network in further education colleges through the provision of learning materials, staff development workshops, regular newsletters and training; setting up and running MARIS-NET, the open learning database for the MSC [now the Training Agency]; research into new areas, for example, Training in Health and Race for the Health Education Council [now HEA] and the Department of Health and Social Security [now the Department of Health and the Department of Social Security]; back up and support for educational television, for example, the BBC 'Computer Literacy' series and the YTV and Channel Four 'Small Business' series.[4]

Ros Morpeth concluded that,

If existing educational providers are going to respond positively to the educational challenges of the future, it is going to be essential to put energy into productive collaboration rather than competition. There is an urgent need for a properly planned and integrated national system of open and distance learning which can only be achieved if existing and new providers are willing to work together constructively (p. 75).

To confirm this view, the NEC began discussions with the Open University to seek to create 'The Learning Company'. In the press release which accompanied the announcement of these discussions Ros Morpeth indicated that such a company would aim to provide

courses which are attractive to a wide range of students, whether they are making their first attempt to return to study, are studying for pleasure, or are preparing to study for a degree or professional qualification. The emphasis of The Learning Company will be on innovation and quality, both of the learning materials and the tutorial and counselling support.

A broadly interpreted 'open learning' potentially has great attractions for the would-be student, who can be given remarkable control – 'Shall I study? If so what shall I study, and how? Where shall I study, and when? What assessment shall I go for, and who will I look to for help and advice?' That such questions can be asked by a potential learner not only suggests considerable individual choice, but also an ability to diagnose needs, to decide what is required in the way of study to meet them, to put together a satisfactory programme and, finally, to be able to evaluate the completed programme.

Such open learning, with its attractive promise of 'autonomy' (i.e. self-governing learners), has led to much innovation since the 1960s in adult education. A good example is provided by Access to Learning for Adults (ALFA), the North London Open College Network. ALFA developed from the running of an 'Access' course by two colleges of further education and a polytechnic. The success of this first initiative was followed by a pilot scheme running an educational advice service in Islington. As the 1987–88 ALFA annual report states, ALFA was set up in the light of 'the further development of trust and perceived benefits to the consumer of working together across sectoral boundaries'. The objectives set were to

> develop links between the institutions that will improve the service offered to adults; identify gaps in provision, encourage the development of courses to fill them and promote progression opportunities; market courses in the colleges that are suitable for adult students; improve advice and counselling to students wishing to return to study in any of the colleges. . . . ALFA holds as fundamental that adults unused or hostile to the educational system should not have to wrestle with the vagaries of an unco-ordinated offer from institutions. If increased access is to be effectively offered then methods of working with and through the providers to improve and extend the offer will have to be found.

ALFA has taken over from SCOPE (Second Chance Opportunities in Education), the now defunct East London Open College Network, and thereby covers Hackney, Islington, Tower Hamlets, and part of Camden.

ALFA has made a substantial contribution to adult education in four main areas, namely information on educational opportunities (e.g. directories of course provision in member institutions, booklets on access and return to learning courses); curriculum development (particularly courses specially designed for adults and linking different sectors of education); staff development; and research and development.

Regarding the latter the CNAA development services briefing of August 1987 is devoted to ALFA's project 'Links into Higher Education' and reports,

> These 'linked courses' are not the same as access courses, jointly developed between FE and HE and with which the polytechnic [of North London] has a more formal relationship. The courses treated here are less formally connected with the HE institution, and are developed initially without polytechnic collaboration. They are: electronics within an independent 'training centre' developing links into the polytechnic's BTEC and degree courses in electronic and communication engineering; an FE 'return to study' course and the polytechnic's social science degree; and women's studies courses in adult education and the polytechnic's part-time degree programme in women's studies. As well as describing the detailed processes involved in establishing these particular 'links', the project's technical report defines such 'links' in relation to other access routes, discusses the reasons for them, describes the courses involved, and suggests a checklist of conditions devised in the course of the negotiations for establishing future 'links'.

In November 1986 at a meeting at the Polytechnic of North London it was decided to set up the National Open College Network. In October 1985 it had been agreed that the possibilities of such a network should be explored, and other meetings had followed. The nine original members were ALFA, the Open College Federation of the North West, Manchester Open College Federation, South Yorkshire Open College, the Open College of South London, Central and West London Open College, the Liverpool Open College Federation, the West Yorkshire Open Learning Federation, and the East London Open College. The network provides a forum to discuss issues of common interest. In a paper for NIACE's Unit for the Development of Adult Continuing Education (UDACE) and its open college networks project Sue Pedder of the London Open College Federation noted:

> Open Colleges share similar aims and concerns but their emphasis and delivery may differ. These aims are to facilitate access and progression into and through education and training for adults,

particularly those whose previous experience of such provision has been disadvantaged, and to make that provision more flexible, accessible and responsive. The delivery of these aims varies in different Open College models. The Open College of the North West (access provided by Stage A and B Units linking Further Education (FE) and Higher Education (HE)), the Manchester Open College Federation model (recognition of courses at 4 levels and accreditation for students' learning) and West Yorkshire Open Learning Federation (5 levels with recognition at levels 1, 2 and 3 delegated to member institutions) have been the main exemplars. Until recently the London systems provided a further variation with no accreditation but education and training providers and agencies linked to facilitate and improve access and progression; London is now well advanced in delivering an accreditation system through the existing Open College Networks along the Manchester model. These models derive from differential local circumstances, origins and initiatives and provide the strong local base for Open Colleges in local areas.

A national open college network has advantages such as making the establishing of credit transfer more easy. In adult education the development of credit transfer has been slower than might be expected with an increasingly mobile population. The ability to combine credit for education and training in one programme and to use it towards a course in another institution or location is a fundamental consideration for any open learning system. At an early stage the network set up a working party to establish a common unit of credit amongst its members and a clear definition of levels of provision.

The National Open College Network's Articles of Association confirm that,

> The principal aims of Associate organisations in the NOCN shall include the facilitation of adults' entry into and progression through post-school education, training and learning in any context; and the provision of services in support of adults returning to learning, particularly those who have been disadvantaged in their previous learning experiences.

In January 1989 UDACE issued its *Adults and the System:*

A Medium Term Strategy for UDACE, which listed in its issues for action 'Balance and Negotiation; Credit Accumulation and Transfer and Modularisation; Inter-Organisational Collaboration; Accreditation; Developing the Notion of Competence; Opening Access to Assessment; Assessment of Institutional Performance; Extending Access to Guidance; and Guidance Processes in the Curriculum'. These priorities largely reflect those found amongst the members of the National Open College Network. The members represent a substantial educational presence; for example, ALFA includes the Hackney Adult Education Institute, the Islington Adult Education Institute, the Tower Hamlets Adult Education Institute, the City and East London College, the City of London Polytechnic, the City University, Hackney College, Kingsway College, North London College, the Polytechnic of North London, Queen Mary College (University of London), the Montefiore Community Education Centre, the Education Advice Service for Islington Adults, Hackney Education Advice Service, Tower Hamlets Education Advice Shop, and the Careers Service. Open colleges are amongst the most important developments in adult education of the last few years.

The most famous of the institutions to use open learning is the Open University (OU), which was created in 1969 to recruit part-time adult students for higher education courses based on distance-teaching methods. The first students registered in 1971 and numbered 19,581 with a median age of 35 years. In 1987 new students registering for undergraduate programmes numbered 16,387 and had a median age of 34 years. In 1971 73 per cent of the undergraduates were male, whilst 54.4 per cent were in 1987. The percentage of disabled students rose from 1.3 to 3.4 over the same period. In 1971 27 per cent had less than two GCE A levels whilst the 1987 figure was 38.9 per cent. England provided 83.9 per cent of undergraduates in 1971 and 83.2 per cent in 1987 (all statistics are from the Open University's *Pocket Guide to OU Figures,* 1988).

From the beginning course teams of scholars from within

and outside the Open University prepared printed correspondence materials which were linked to OU television and radio programmes broadcast by the BBC. In 1971 4.5 hours of television per week and 4.5 hours of radio were transmitted; by 1987 these had risen to 22.1 hours of television and 6 hours of radio. There were set books, some of which had been specially commissioned by the OU. Some face-to-face teaching and advice was available from student counsellors in the 260 study centres established in 1971 (the figure is the same for 1987). England was divided into ten regions, each served by a regional office; Scotland, Wales and Northern Ireland each have a regional office.

From the beginning the OU's general degrees were based on a credit system where four credits gave a pass degree and eight an honours degree. Up to three credits could be claimed for other qualifications. Normally students managed a credit in a year, but were allowed to take up to two credits per annum. For a number of programmes, such as the foundation course, there has always been a compulsory one-week summer school normally held on the campus of another university.

The Open University asks for no formal entrance qualifications. Undergraduate places are allocated according to regional quotas and to availability of arts, social science, education, mathematics, science, and technology courses. As with all such efforts to open up the educational system, those with more experience of education have always been more likely to be able to exploit the opportunities within the OU than the early school-leaver with his or her lack of knowledge and often poor self-confidence.

The Open University has always received most of its finance from the Department of Education and Science (DES). In 1987 the DES recurrent grant was £62.3 million, whilst student fees provided £21.4 million, and other sources £5.8 million. Expenditure was made up of £21 million on academic and research; £19.9 million on teaching (including summer schools) and regional services; £9.6 million on the BBC; £12.6 million on administration; £6 million on estates; £7.3 million on continuing education; and £200,000 on 'other'. In 1971 the tuition fee was £20 and the summer school fee £25; this had risen in 1987 to £158 and £103 respectively. As assistance to OU students by local education authorities is discretionary, most hard-pressed authorities do not help with course fees. Since its inception a major problem for the Open University has been students dropping out because of the cost of the programmes.

After the success of the undergraduate courses the OU inevitably began to offer other provision. In 1976 only six higher degrees were awarded, but by 1987 this had risen to 127, of which 55 were PhDs. In 1987 there were 6,464 BA graduates. In January 1975 the OU's Council set up a Committee on Continuing Education under Sir Peter Venables to look at the OU's potential contribution:

> the Committee has deliberately excluded consideration of the education of 16 and 17 year olds, as well as of higher education which follows on without a break after schooling has ceased. We have therefore chosen to focus attention on education for adults which is normally resumed after a break or interruption, often involving a period in employment. The undergraduate programme of the Open University itself is also largely excluded from this report.[5]

The report included a long list of recommendations in such areas as educational advice and counselling, preparatory courses, adult concern courses, materials and accreditation, tutor training, and professional and vocational courses and materials.

In 1980 the Open University's interim delegacy for continuing education published *A Plan for the Development of Continuing Education*, which stated that

> The University's contribution to continuing education should be seen in a national, not in an institutional context. It will need to be set in the context of two broad national trends. Firstly, the growing expectation that educational provision should be directed at meeting the changing needs of society; the need for technical or professional updating, the possibility of more frequent career/job change, the probability of greater uncommitted (if not leisure)

time, the need for the individual to understand issues about, for example, the environment or wealth creation and to develop personal effectiveness in the family and community. Secondly, growing concern for continuing education generally has meant that many other providers are properly involved in teaching and learning systems which are distance-based and which make use of the media exploited by the Open University. Major unions, broadcasting agents, industries and academic validators are already developing directed private study or open learning systems and are also exploiting educational and media technology. Many are finding, as we do, that the creation of the materials is only one part of the process. The effective provision of educational opportunities at local level is still a major problem awaiting dynamic solutions.

The Centre for Continuing Education was established in the same year.

There were fourteen specially prepared continuing education courses in 1976 (with 4,640 students) and 126 in 1987 (13,190 students). Associate students (those taking courses which are part of the undergraduate programme but as separate elements) numbered 4,578 in 1976 and 11,734 in 1987. In 1988 the university's continuing education programme had some 150 courses, 20,000 students, and sold over 67,000 information packs. The Open Business School whch was started in 1983 had 8,800 students in 1988, whilst the Scientific and Technological Updating programme claimed 1,500, Professional Development in Education 900 students, Health and Social Welfare 7,100, Community Education 2,300, and Personal and Cultural Education 120. In its brief on Scientific and Technological Updating the OU states,

As its contribution to the national drive to modernise British industry, the Open University has inroduced a range of courses which will help managers, scientists and engineers to update existing knowledge or enter new fields. In association with the Science and Engineering Research Council (SERC) the University has launched two programmes of short courses, one concerned with manufacturing and the other with industrial applications of computers. Among the subjects covered are manufacturing systems, quality systems and techniques, robotics, computer-aided engineering, software engineering, and computer architectures and operating systems. The courses are modular and credits can be built up for a postgraduate diploma or, with the addition of a dissertation, a postgraduate MSc degree. Other courses and packs deal with such subjects as computing, electronics, biotechnology and agriculture.

In its 1989–91 Scientific and Technological Updating Plans the Open University proposes that it should create an institute 'specialising in training and updating services to industry in order to capitalise on the expanding market opportunities and Sector/University strengths', but warns that 'substantial external funding would be essential for the creation of such an Institute'.

In June 1989 the final report of the steering group for the academic review entitled *The Open University into the 1990s* was produced for presentation to the university's academic board in July 1989, which then passed it to other bodies for consideration and implementation. The fundamental objectives of the Open University are listed as openness ('student access to, and study within, the university not being hampered because of age, gender, race, disability, economic circumstance, previous educational attainment, geographical location within the UK or preferred course of study'), quality, and breadth (to 'meet a variety of intellectual, professional and vocational needs').

Many of the report's recommendations relate to the problems of resourcing. England has a chronically underfinanced educational service, and the Open University reflects this. As recommendation 2 notes,

> The University should develop a policy on pricing for the non-undergraduate programmes which achieves maximum income in some areas, in order to maintain openness in the undergraduate programme, and in those parts of the non-undergraduate programme where the principle of openness is paramount.

Recommendation 16 proposes that

> The University must, as a matter of urgency, make easier the task

of students beginning study with the OU by some combination of: reviewing the current foundation courses from the standpoint of length, start date, skills acquisition, pacing, and accessibility to returning students; developing access courses, possibly in collaboration with other agencies; developing a programme whereby the time between registration and the beginning of the foundation courses, or beginning courses in other programmes, can be used more constructively.

Recommendation 17 states

The University should expand its range of professional and vocational training and updating, especially by exploiting much more systematically the resources available in its undergraduate programme. It also must look for ways to strengthen its competitive position in the areas of: face-to-face tuition; training orientated specifically to local customers.

Recommendation 31 suggests, 'Active consideration should be given to the location of study centres in community centres, workplaces and other venues, as well as in the premises of other providers of higher education'. Recommendation 38 proposes that

The University should seek to collaborate with other providers but each potential collaborative project should be subject to prior evaluation to establish whether it wll bring clear advantages in maintaining existing areas of OU provision, or in extending the University's programmes of study as specified in academic plans.

The OU's recurrent financial crises during the 1980s have emphasised its cautious instincts. It will fill a middle-of-the-road role in higher education during the 1990s as it has done from its foundation in 1969. Its contribution will be of vital importance to an inadequate higher-education provision in England, but it is unlikely to pioneer new directions in adult education. This comes through clearly in the 1989 report. As the charter of the university states, its objectives are

the advancement and dissemination of learning and knowledge by teaching and research by a diversity of means such as broadcasting and technological devices appropriate to higher education, by correspondence tuition, residential courses and seminars and in other relevant ways ... to provide education of University and professional standards for its students and to promote the educational well-being of the community generally.

Such admirable objectives are likely to inspire technical innovation, but not necessarily curriculum innovation. The Open University will expand its activities and reach audiences at present undervalued by other areas of higher and further education.

This is not a criticism, but an acknowledgement of the Open University's original framework, which has been emphasised further by national financial restraint. The Open University is about successful provision for a wide audience, but its structure and style is not about innovation. Its Community Education Academic Plan for 1989–91, where new ideas might most be expected, confirms this. The proposals are excellent, and of prime importance to the country's well-being, but are developments of others' innovations, whether the Community Action Learning Programme, with its aims of building self-confidence, facilitating a return to learning, training and work, and developing local communities, or 'Living with AIDS', or 'Life Management Skills', or its diploma in community education. The Open University is a superb distance-education institution delivering excellent courses and dealing in, for English higher education, rarely equalled numbers. It has confirmed a large, unsatisfied demand for higher and further education and helped to satisfy at least part of it with very good programmes.

In his students' guide produced for the Council of Educational Technology under the title *How to Win as an Open Learner* (1986), Phil Race gives an exhaustive list of decisions the open learner should be able to make:

Where to learn? When to learn? What to learn? How fast to learn? How much to learn? Whether to have your learning tested? How to have your learning tested? Whether to use the help of a tutor? Whether to work wth fellow learners? Whether to do any practical or 'hands-on' work? Whether to decide to give up learning? Whether to bother to start at all?

Roger Lewis, director of the Corporate Services Division of the Open College in an article in *Training Technology* (April 1988) entitled 'The Open College and Industry' stated that the Open College has to satisfy five criteria. These show the importance in practice of the questions posed by Phil Race:

> training must be available at times that suit employer and employee; training must be available in places that suit employer and employee – whether at work, at home or in a special training location; training must be available in short chunks, to fit easily into company and employee work schedules; training must be relevant to the work place; the training outcomes agreed with employers; standards of performance achieved through taking Open College courses must be nationally recognised.

Whilst not being as 'open' as Race's questions would assume, the Open College has many of the characteristics associated with open learning.

Contributing to 'On Air/Off Air' in 1989, the chief executive of the Open College, Sheila Innes, confirmed that

> The primary objective of The Open College in 1989 is to move rapidly towards becoming a profitable company committed to offering its clients, both individual and corporate, a means of achieving lasting, quantifiable improvement in performance through the provision of high quality, flexible, vocational training materials and services. . . . It is clear that the College will place more emphasis in future on its work for the corporate sector – industry and commerce – and make every effort to reach individuals through their workplace (as well as, where appropriate, through special schemes for those seeking work). The College has learnt, over the past 12 months, that its 'total package approach' to companies of all sizes has special appeal for busy employers whose aim is to offer high quality, affordable, flexible training through both materials and support, on site. Each course needs to cater for that particular company's needs. The course must be 'customised' as opposed to generic. The College has therefore developed a Corporate Services Division, which includes provision of training needs analysis, courses selection, customisation and delivery.

The Open College's use of 'in-house centres' is aimed at

tailoring responses to each company's or individual's unique needs. It is based on a range of advice to would-be users on which programmes would meet their needs, the allocation of a mentor for advice and encouragement, involvement of a line manager to assist in the learners' application of their new knowledge and skills to job tasks, easy access to the rest of the company and its staff, plenty of information on progress, and the prompt answering of the learners' questions.

The in-house centre within a company provides information on Open College programmes, support to learners using the Open College's packages in a variety of ways, and ensures effective information links with the Open College. The firm receives the Open College's marketing support, guidance materials, newsletters, course materials, access to a hotline, new course previews, and price negotiations. Such companies as Jaguar, B & Q, and ICI, with their well-known commitment to training, quickly took advantage of the Open College's in-house centres concept.

The Open College will find it much harder to interest companies throughout the English economy because of a culture less enthusiastic about training than that of the United States, West Germany, or Japan. The government's anxiety to make the Open College financially self-sufficient in as short a period as possible is both unrealistic and shortsighted. The Germans have had a State interest in training since they began to industrialise at the second stage of the industrial revolution in the nineteenth century. As the first industrial country Britain was uniquely creative, but inevitably had an *ad hoc* approach to training. The traditional English belief that governments should try to maintain a hands-off attitude means that the Open College is yet another institution battling against a long and contrary set of values which inhibits State commitment to educational investment and which encourages companies to take training less seriously than do their international rivals. In the field of vocational adult education the Open College is an initiative of singular importance, but it will take several years to make a full impact. It will be unfortunate if the Open College finds itself expending too much energy in trying to interest overseas buyers in its courses in order to balance its budget. The crisis is over our inadequately trained workforce, which is where all the Open College's enthusiasm should be directed. It is not meant to solve this problem for other countries.

Sheila Innes confirms that

> The objective of all OC courses and services is to increase performance on the job. National qualifications will continue to set standards and be nationally available. The development of National Vocational Qualifications will enable OC courses to be developed to an appropriate competence-based standard in line with national progress towards cumulative, transferable credit and Records of Achievement for learners, a useful testimonial for future employers, and tangible evidence of acquired skills. Quality, in all aspects of what we do, is our aim. A set of rigorous procedures, including market research, employer advice, tendering and detailed project control ensure that OC courses are among the best and in some cases unique e.g. a 120 hour multi-media course for care support workers leading to a City and Guilds Certificate (325). Similarly the College has developed a stringent criteria checklist for buy-ins; minimum services are specified in our contracts for support, so that Open Access Centres throughout the land provide learners with effective counselling and tutorial support. A major advance in ensuring competence in this area, and also inside companies, is the development with RSA, City and Guilds and Scotvec of COLD, the first Certificate in Open Learning Delivery. ('On Air, Off Air', 1989)

The Open College again highlights the fast development of open learning systems in the 1980s. With its regional offices for the Midlands, North-East, North-West, Home Counties North, Home Counties South, South-West, and Wales its impact on vocational adult education will be substantial. The Training Agency's open learning branch also augurs well for such approaches. In 1987 it stated that its new programme would aim at further development of the open learning infrastructure, the extension of delivery networks and supply, more training for trainers, the dissemination of experience, codes of practice and quality assurance mechanisms, more help for small firms, incentives on a 50:50 basis for industry to use open learning, the development of materials directed at certain groups such as high-level skill shortage areas and help with disadvantaged groups, and the creation of an open learning directory comprehensively covering vocational open-learning materials and services.

In April 1988 the National Council for Educational Technology was formed by the amalgamation of the Council for Educational Technology (CET) and the Microelectronics Education Support Unit. Under its chief executive, it aims to promote the use of technological developments in all areas of education, and to introduce such educational initiatives into industry and the public services. It has a commitment to the encouragement of new approaches to learning, and is involved in the development of new systems of instruction. In open learning it has published such seminal texts as W. J. K. Davies's *Towards Autonomy in Learning: Process or Product?* (1987), Vernon Smith's *Public Libraries and Adult Independent Learners* (1987) and Dorothea Hall's *Adult Learning by Choice* (1986). When the Manpower Services Commission published in 1985 its consultative document. *The Future Development of Open Learning* the Council for Educational Technology's response illustrated one of its great strengths, which is to take a long-term view, something at which the contemporary English are not good.

CET is concerned that the MSC paper ignores the real challenge which underlies all consideration of the future of open learning in that it misinterprets the time-scale involved. It heads para 12 with the words 'Development to the end of the decade': this is a frighteningly short-term view. In CET's view, we are now at the stage where we should be considering the developments which will need to be undertaken during the next five to ten year period in order that there shall be a system of vocational education and training in place by 1995 which will be appropriate to national needs at that time. What sort of system might this be? We should suggest: it should take account of those technologies which we can, today, see will be widely available and which allow the concepts of open access and learner controlled learning to move a stage further. Because vocational education and training must offer very diverse and flexible provision in order to match national and individual needs, there can be no question of a rigid national framework. Rather, we shall need to define the functions to be provided and the techniques and technologies which can be used to provide them. We then need to work out a broad based development plan, involving all those whose expertise can contribute to its successful implementation, which will lead to the provision of these functions on a national and comprehensive scale. Examples of the functions which will need to be provided include: a generally accessible guidance and information system, since every user of training will need guidance in identifying needs and the ways of satisfying them; a modular system of vocational education and training with transferable credits within a nationally recognised system of awards; definition of the communications facilities which the trainees may be expected to be able to access (especially in order to avoid continued reliance on out-dated methods). These types of functions will need to be provided without the need for all training to be provided in similar, centrally determined packages, originating in one organisation or distributed through one channel. Similarly, provision will need to be made for adult students of all types (without the present artificial limitation to technician, supervisory and managerial categories).[6]

Without a doubt such views have influenced the direction of English open-learning provision in the area of vocational adult education. Both government and private initiatives have made the latter a sector of education of enhanced activity and innovation. There is often a fruitful interchange of ideas, research findings and practice between vocational and non-vocational adult education. A DES-sponsored agency such as the Further Education Unit (FEU), established to promote, encourage and develop the efficient provision of further education in Britain, finds itself contributing to both vocational and non-vocational adult education, as we have seen with its research project RP460, 'Adults in the Colleges of Further Education'. The FEU has co-operated with the DES and Welsh Office funded REPLAN programme based at the National Institute of Adult Continuing Education and created to promote the development of educational opportunities for the adult unemployed. Such a joint venture was FEU research project RP417 ('The Outreach College: Design and Implementation', 1989) which looked at the most appropriate ways of taking further education and training out into the community. REPLAN uses many familiar vehicles for spreading ideas and information such as a team of regional field officers, national and regional conferences, newsletters, bulletins, exhibitions, and research reports. Within adult education open learning has been part of an increasingly professional approach to information-giving.

Notes

1 N. Paine (ed.) *Open Learning in Transition* (National Extension College, 1988), p. xi.
2 R. Freeman, *The National Extension College: Its Aims and Development* (Open University, 1983).
3 J. Jenkins and H. D. Perraton, *The Invisible College: National Extension College 1963–1979* (International Extension College, Cambridge, 1980), pp. 65–6.
4 In *Open Learning in Transition* (see note 1).
5 *Report of the Committee on Continuing Education* (December 1976), p. 6.
6 Council for Educational Technology, *Annual Report* (1986), pp. 80–1.

Chapter 6

THE LOCAL EDUCATION AUTHORITIES AND NON-VOCATIONAL ADULT EDUCATION

The Education Reform Act 1988 makes no reference to adult education. In the House of Lords on 7 July 1988, on behalf of the government, Baroness Hooper confirmed that the term 'further education' covered all those over the age of 16 years. Without a doubt the Act increases the power of the Secretary of State and will give local education authorities less direct control of the education service as institutions act with greater autonomy. The position of non-vocational adult education within local education authorities over the coming years could be a matter of some concern. With an annual enrolment in England and Wales of approaching 2 million students, non-vocational adult education within the LEAs is of importance to our national well-being.

In a thoughtful document entitled *Adults and the Act* (1988) the Unit for the Development of Adult Continuing Education at NIACE posed several key questions arising from the Act for the consideration of local education authorities:

What kind of policy and planning framework does the Authority intend to create in order to set a context for its schemes of financial delegation and government? How will the Authority describe an 'adequate' service? What steps will be taken to identify the needs to be met and what level of provision will be made available in response to those needs? What mechanisms does the Authority intend to create in order to coordinate its planning with that of other providing agencies, including voluntary and private agencies? Is the present structure of institutions [FE, HE, AE, CE and

Tertiary] appropriate for the delivery of adequate and equitable provision, or does the Authority wish to change the way in which the institutions providing education for adults are organised? Should governing bodies be created for all institutions providing for adults, and if so how should they be constituted? In allocating resources to institutions under the scheme of financial delegation what arrangements does the Authority plan to make for recognising the costs of adult provision, bearing in mind the relatively high costs of part-time, open learning and evening provision? Does the Authority intend to 'earmark' resources within delegated FE budgets in order to secure the survival of particular kinds of provision for adults? How does the Authority intend to ensure that 'school' premises currently used by adults remain accessible and that the powers of governing bodies to control premises do not conflict with the duty of the LEAs to secure provision? How does the Authority intend to ensure that the costing of shared premises (particularly premises shared with schools – LEA and grant maintained) is properly identified and allocated? Are there cases where 'surplus' school accommodation is currently being used in the day-time but might revert to school use under open entry provisions for school pupils? Are there measures which the Authority should take to safeguard this position? Does the Authority intend, and in what way, to restrict the power of school governing bodies to provide education for adults? What arrangements does the Authority intend to make to ensure the continuation of joint courses, where adults and school pupils are taught together? Are there staff currently employed on joint adult/school or adult/FE contracts whose position may be endangered by the new powers of governing bodies to dismiss staff? What arrangements will the Authority propose to secure adult use of premises in schools which become Grant Maintained? How does the Authority intend to ensure the continuation and development of effective links for adult students moving from FE to HE (including Access courses and Open College Networks)? How does the Authority see the role of its adult educators in developing or mounting training for school governors? How does the Authority see the role of its adult educators in helping parents and other members of the community to understand the implications of the changes taking place in the education system?

Such questions not only form an impressive and cogent

review of the 1988 Act from the viewpoint of a particularly vulnerable sector of English education, but also say much about the present provision of non-vocational adult education. For example, obviously unlike Japanese social education (the rough equivalent) with its magnificent nationwide network of purpose built *kominkan* (centres), English non-vocational adult education mainly meets in schools and similar buildings belonging to other people. Whilst the former Inner London Education Authority took its non-vocational adult education very seriously, as a relatively rich authority might, and provided adult education institutes (Camden, City Lit, Clapham–Battersea, Fulham and Chelsea, Hackney, Hammersmith and North Kensington, Islington, Lambeth, Mary Ward Centre, Morley College, Putney and Wandsworth, Ravensbourne, South Greenwich, South Lewisham, Southwark, Streatham and Tooting, Thamesside, Tower Hamlets, Westminster, and the Working Men's College),[1] most other local education authorities do not.

As Derek Legge's authoritative book *The Education of Adults in Great Britain* demonstrated, there is a rich variety of approaches to non-vocational adult education in England, and this is as true of the local education authority sector as elsewhere.[2] Some authorities favour using colleges of further education as a base for their non-vocational adult education, whilst others use school buildings during the evenings. Some LEAs have accepted the Cambridge village college model and have community colleges which contain both school and adult education (often called community schools). Often an authority will have a mixture of adult education models which have developed over the years with some self-contained adult education centres alongside the use of school buildings in the evenings and some more recent community schools.

In non-vocational adult education over 70 per cent of the students in most authorities' provision are women. Most classes take place during the evening, but an increasing proportion (perhaps 30 per cent) in recent years have met in the daytime. The range of subjects on offer in Inner London's *Floodlight* guide to part-time day and evening classes for

1989–90 is impressive, covering 282 pages in its alphabetical listing. For example, under 'A' there are classes in access, accountancy, acoustics, acrobatics, advertising, advice, African studies, Afro-Caribbean studies, AIDS, aikido, air conditioning, air pollution control, alarm systems, Alexander method, alternative medicine, amateur radio, American studies, Amharic, anatomy, ancestor tracing, ancient Egypt, ancient world, angling, animals, animation, anthropology, anti-racism and feminism, antiques, Arabic, archaeology, archery, architecture, arithmetic, aromatherapy, art, Asian studies, asphalting, assertiveness training, astrology, astronomical navigation, astronomy, athletics, auctioneering and estate management, audio-typewriting, audio-visual, automobile engineering, and aviation. It represents a tradition of unusual social and intellectual richness which has developed over the past century or so. Of course the range of such provision in the former ILEA areas would not be matched by non-vocational adult education in less highly populated areas, or by those LEAs with fewer resources or less commitment to the service.

Colin Griffith writes:

In theory, liberal adult educators tend to justify redistributive state interference in terms of the democratic virtue and collective benefit of educated, informed, and participative citizens. In practice, the economics of the marketplace have located the burden of payment for liberal and recreative education much more on the consumer, reflecting a Thatcherite but perhaps not unduly cynical view that people who consume liberal adult education probably benefit as individuals and thus should pay the full market price. In short, the market model, increasingly invoked by the government for traditional liberal adult education, assumes that it is not the business of the state to subsidize learning that meets individual needs as such.[3]

Efforts to challenge such views have met with varying degrees of success, but overall there has been a notable decline in the State's and local government's subsidy to non-vocational adult education since 1979.

Whilst most local education authorities take administrative

and financial control of their non-vocational adult education programmes, other matters (such as the curriculum) are usually in the hands of full-time or part-time professional adult educators in consultation with various interested parties, notably the consumers. Many adult studies departments in colleges of further education, community colleges, or adult centres have a student organisation which will have some say in the decisions made. This ranges from a nominal sharing of power between the professional adult educator and the students' committee to rare examples of institutions largely run by their students.

Many LEAs have a short-term residential college as part of their non-vocational adult education service, which provides short courses of one to fourteen days' duration. The Lancashire College for Adult Education in Chorley is unusual in that it has modern purpose-built accommodation for 51 people to stay overnight. Alston Hall College near Preston is more typical in that it was a former coal-mine owner's nineteenth-century mansion. It accommodates 45 students and is notable for its residential courses in literature, music, art, drama, history and philosophy. Knuston Hall in Northamptonshire is in a historic building at Irchester and has residential accommodation for 57. Lincolnshire's Horncastle Residential College is in carefully modified post-war buildings originally constructed for other purposes and can take 82 students. Whilst local education authorities' financial stringency in recent years has seen the closure of a number of short-term residential colleges, they remain an important regional and national adult education resource increasingly used for courses for industry, commerce and public bodies as well as for non-vocational adult education for the general public. They are found from the Devon Centre for Continuing Education at Totnes to Cumbria's Higham Hall at Bassenthwaite Lake.

The previously mentioned Educational Centres Association established in 1921 represents about 150 adult education institutions (students and staff) ranging from Ashby de la Zouch's Ivanhoe Community College to Woking and Chertsey

Adult Education Institute in Surrey. As the association stated in its response to the 1989 government's efficiency scrutiny, those in the centres it represents account for a fifth of all students in non-vocational adult education. The association aims at promoting a partnership between those who provide such courses and those who attend. All its committees have strong student representation (e.g. the key executive committee is constitutionally obliged to have half its membership made up of students), and the association is the only one which gives such priority to the relationship between students and providers. The association's major purpose is the promotion and well-being of adult education, with its underpinning belief that this is part of fulfilling the needs of the individual and of society as a whole. Amongst its many roles that of being an effective lobbying agency for non-vocational adult education has been amongst the most important.

Although work with the less advantaged of English society has long been a tradition in adult education, the 1973 Russell Report gave it greater formal prominence. The rapid increase in the number of unemployed adults in the later 1970s saw many local education authorities encouraging adult educators to make special provision or give easier access to such students. A good example is provided by Nottinghamshire County Council's booklet, *Access for the Unemployed*, with eight sections covering employment, education, leisure, volunteering, child care, welfare rights advice, your county councillors, and other useful addresses. The education section has short descriptions of what is available, from adult basic education to higher education. The brief piece about Clarendon College of Further Education represents well the style of approach and what is on offer:

> Whatever sort of education or training you want, Clarendon College can supply it or will put you in touch with someone who can. Contact. . . . You can get advice and guidance, leaflets and further details on courses. All courses are free to the unemployed and there is a creche available every day at a small cost. The main College is close to the city centre and is easily reached by bus. There are also several other centres which may be closer to your

home, and you can even choose some courses which you do exactly where and when you decide.

Most adult education centres are run by a professional principal or area organiser. Usually they have been trained as schoolteachers, often starting their adult education experience as part-timers earning extra money to supplement their teacher's salary. Such full-time adult education principals are administrators, running their programme and accommodation with modest clerical assistance. Whilst most LEAs will have some advisory staff for non-vocational adult education, some do not have this extra support for overworked principals.

In her study *Adults Learning*, Jennifer Rogers observed:

> Many teachers of adults work in total isolation from one another. They earn insultingly small amounts of money. They teach in wildly unsuitable rooms. They have virtually no special training. The petty frustrations of their teaching environments can often seem overwhelming when it is combined with inexperience and lack of readily available advice.[4]

Whilst most LEAs have improved training opportunities for part-time teachers and there has been some modest increase in tutor fees, non-vocational adult education remains a low priority. The general public has given it increasing support since the Second World War, but underfunded local education authorities have been forced to give priority to their clearly defined mandatory obligations. Adult education classes still mainly use other people's buildings, rely on part-time teaching staff, and face ever-increasing fee levels. There are some more favoured areas of provision, such as classes in literacy and numeracy or those for ethnic minorities, but this is often a matter of modest differences (a lower fee for an adult literacy class than for dressmaking or keep fit, for example).

Adult basic education

Adult basic education was given a boost by the Russell Report and the British Association of Settlements' 'Right to Read' campaign of the early 1970s. Under pressure the government of the day in 1975 set up the Adult Literacy Resource Agency (ALRA) under the aegis of the National Institute of Adult Education (as it then was). ALRA published teaching materials, aided voluntary bodies, encouraged and sponsored training, and appointed full-time staff which were then assigned to LEAs.

The adult literacy provision in the ALRA years mainly relied on unpaid, voluntary tutors (some 80,000 volunteers in the first five years) who taught on a one-to-one basis, meeting their student in either their own or the student's home. The one-to-one teaching declined substantially during the 1980s as tutors and organisers increasingly preferred groups to meet in educational centres. After three years ALRA was replaced by the Adult Literacy Unit (ALU), which was given a two-year life. By the end of the two years perhaps 160,000 people in England and Wales had received literacy tuition during the ALRA–ALU period. In 1980 the ALU was succeeded by the Adult Literacy and Basic Skills Unit (ALBSU), whose brief was to contribute to 'literacy and numeracy and those related basic communication and coping skills, without which people are impeded from applying or being considered for employment'. The expanded remit from that given to the ALU partly reflected the proposals from the Advisory Council for Adult and Continuing Education's 1979 report *A Strategy for the Basic Education of Adults*. In 1985 ALBSU was placed on a three-year rolling programme. Its DES and Welsh Office grant by 1988–89 was over £2.5 million for

> developing within the general education service in England and Wales provision designed to improve the standards of proficiency for adults, whose first or second language is English, in the areas of communication and coping skills without which progress in and towards education, training, or employment is impeded.

The ALBSU saw English as a second language for adults added to its brief during the 1980s. English for speakers of other languages (ESOL) has fitted into ALBSU's contribution more comfortably than might have been expected.

Since the relatively modest beginnings of the adult literacy campaign of the late 1960s and early 1970s it has become a diverse and impressive part of adult education with local authorities, the Training Agency and voluntary agencies substantially involved. The quality of provision has improved notably, and the ALBSU can take much of the credit, for its consultancy and advisory service to LEAs and others, its sponsorship of development projects, the quality of its teaching and learning materials, the tradition of regional and national staff training, its funding of key areas of research, and its ability to keep basic education in the limelight and, notably, in the consciousness of key ministers. The 1989 ALBSU annual conference was addressed by Norman Fowler, the Secretary of State for Employment, whilst the previous year's conference had listened to Kenneth Baker, then Secretary of State for Education and Science.

The ALBSU newsletters for spring and summer 1989 illustrate well the range of its present interests. The spring number includes articles entitled 'How Special are Special Needs?', 'Basic Skills Accreditation Initiative', 'Numeracy – Abstract Art or Basically Boring?', 'Setting Up an Open Learning Centre', and an insert on 'Making Reading Easier'. The summer edition has a four-page insert on 'Initial Interview and Assessment in ESOL', and articles on 'Employment Training: Co-operation or Competition?', 'Literacy for the Workplace', 'Desktop Publishing for Adult Literacy', and 'Making a Start with Computers'. The newsletters each carry short reviews of books and other materials covering four pages. Publishers have signalled the comparatively rapid growth in adult basic education by their interest in it.

Although the ALBSU operates as an agency of the National Institute of Adult Continuing Education with its major commitment still to work with the local education authorities, its other activities are diverse. Institutions within adult education are now less isolationist than perhaps previously was the case. Not only are interests in an area of provision increasingly shared but so, often, are resources.

Prison education

A fast-growing area of adult education provision since the Second World War which relies heavily on its partnership with the local education authorities is HM Prison Service. This comes under the Home Office and has a chief education officer aided by six principal education officers (two based at HQ and one each for the south-west region, northern region, south-east region, and midlands region) and four senior education officers. Every prison, young offenders' institution, and remand centre has an education officer who is an employee of the LEA. Whilst most teaching is by part-time tutors, there are some full-time teachers and deputy education officers. Between 1982 and 1987 there was a 17 per cent increase in salaried teaching staff and the ratio of full-time to part-time teachers is rising. A number of local education authorities have established units within their colleges of further education to give prison education staff better access to colleagues, resources and staff development. Of the 123 education units in HM Prison Service, 110 now have a relationship with a college of further education or an adult education institute.

Programmes are made up of remedial, academic, social, cultural, recreational and vocational education (vocational training courses are staffed by instructors who are civil servants). As provision is through the LEAs, it largely reflects further education/adult education developments outside the prisons. The *Report of the Work of the Prison Service April 1987 to March 1988* showed that in 1986–87 60,000 inmates were tested for literacy and that over 40 per cent of teaching resources were devoted to basic education. 1986–87 saw a 5 per cent increase in total student hours to 6.5 million (hours spent in education classes were in excess of 5.3 million whilst vocational-training student hours reached 1.28 million).

The National Educational Services Consultative Committee (ESCC) was reviewed and reorganised, and in 1987 a working party was set up to examine the relationship between the prison service and the LEAs, which reported to ESCC in

1989. As there had previously been no written agreement between the LEAs and HM Prison Service regarding education this had led to considerable regional variations in provision. Such unevenness suggests that a written agreement needs to be drawn up so that each side knows exactly what is expected of it.

The decision in 1989 to second four NVQ development officers to advise prison governors on the implications of the National Council for Vocational Qualifications should lead to further cohesion in prison education and training. Other developments are likely to have a similar effect, such as the use of self-evaluation so that local management can systematically assess its provision, a programme of management training courses for education officers, and progress towards a nationally agreed curriculum framework. The latter would help overcome the problem of disrupted education caused by the increasing tendency to move inmates around.

The relationship between the local education authorities and HM Prison Service in the field of education has been of mutual benefit. Prison education has been quick to take up new ideas; for example it has set up five information technology centres at Ashwell, Sudbury, Leyhill, East Sutton Park and Kirkham, each with a national responsibility for some aspect such as videotex or information systems. It also has a good reputation for carrying out research and development, for example the development of its own databases including one in open learning. LEAs have benefited too, from information and access to ideas and resources. Any institution with a strong and distinct culture, such as HM Prison Service, is in danger of isolation and the local education authorities' partnership has helped to avoid this.

The National Institute of Adult Continuing Education

The National Institute has a constitution which gives its objective as the advancement of adult continuing education. It offers consultation, advice and information to organisations and individuals. It pursues research and enquiries, publishes journals for the field, and books and directories such as the

Year Book of Adult Continuing Education. It organises conferences and seminars, and operates a computerised database of bibliographical information. As already noted it hosts the Unit for the Development of Adult Continuing Education (UDACE), a major element of the DES adult unemployed programme in REPLAN, and the Adult Literacy and Basic Skills Unit. The funding of such units in each case is greater than that of NIACE itself. There is also a Wales Committee NIACE/NIACE Cymru based in Cardiff. NIACE's headquarters is in Leicester.

Although NIACE has a strong association with the local education authorities it is a genuinely 'national' institution. The membership of its council illustrates this, ranging from representatives of the Association of County Councils through such bodies as the Field Studies Council and the board of education of the Church of England General Synod and the Society of Industrial Tutors, to the National Association of Teachers in Further and Higher Education. Below the council there is a smaller executive committee and a finance and general purposes sub-committee. Various other sub-committees cover conferences and international services, research library and information services, publications, women's education, ethnic minorities, and special needs. Funding for the National Institute comes largely from local education authority sources and the DES and Welsh Office. For an institute speaking on behalf of a very wealthy country of approaching 50 million people in the key area of adult education, NIACE is slimly financed. From such a modest funding base over the years it has made a substantial impact on the quality and direction of English adult education. Its research and publications, often backed up by effective conferences to disseminate information and ideas, have regularly helped to put on the national agenda such issues as student fee levels, adult literacy, paid educational leave and a score of other topics, from Alexandra Withnall's *The Christian Churches and Adult Education* (NIACE, 1986) to the seminal *Adult Education: Adequacy of Provision* (NIACE, 1970).[5]

Of parallel importance has been the National Institute's

international links. No country can afford to be insular in a world where change and innovation are the only permanent features. NIACE has fed into English adult education information on ideas and practices from abroad which have greatly aided the field. Similarly, it has spread abroad knowledge of English provision and developments which has aided other systems. NIACE has helped to found or warmly supported a number of international associations such as the European Bureau of Adult Education, the International Council for Adult Education, and the Commonwealth Association for the Education and Training of Adults.

Notes

1 *Floodlight* (1989–90), p. 26.
2 D. Legge, *The Education of Adults in Great Britain* (Open University Press, 1982).
3 'Continuing Education and Social Policy' in P. Jarvis (ed.) *Britain: Policy and Practice in Continuing Education* (Jossey-Bass, 1988), p. 16.
4 J. Rogers, *Adults Learning* (Penguin, 1971), p. 194.
5 On fee levels, see the annual surveys by Alan Charnley and Veronica McGivney (NIACE); on adult literacy see, for example, H. A. Jones and A. Charnley, *Adult Literacy – A Study of its Impact* (NIACE, 1977); and on paid educational leave, see J. Killeen and M. Bird, *Education and Work: A Study of Paid Educational Leave in England and Wales* (1976/77) (NIACE, 1981).

Chapter 7

THE UNIVERSITIES, THE WORKERS' EDUCATIONAL ASSOCIATION AND BROADCASTING

The universities

When I first attended a Universities Council for Adult Education (UCAE; later the Universities Council for Adult and Continuing Education, UCACE) conference in the 1960s it was an organisation of extra-mural department directors (often called 'the barons'). This was still the case when I went to Nottingham as professor of adult education in 1974, although change was very much in the air. The non-vocational adult education traditions which formally began with Cambridge in 1873, and were reinforced by the establishing of many university departments of adult education or extra-mural studies in the inter-war period and immediately after the Second World War, were still dominant in the early 1970s with UCAE giving off something of the air of a club of directors of extra-mural studies. Since then the universities' rapidly increasing interest in vocational adult education has seen UCACE joined by the directors of new units devoted to such work, and the development of substantial vocational adult education programmes within the established departments of adult education.

There has been a notable increase in post-experience vocational education (PEVE) in universities, beginning in the 1980s. Some departments and faculties, such as medicine and education, have long had a strong tradition in this field, but new initiatives like PICKUP and further interest amongst consumers beset by rapid new developments and information have made PEVE a priority for the first time in all English universities. As the Secretary of State noted in his lecture to a conference at Lancaster University on 5 January 1989

> In modern societies the universities, polytechnics and colleges of higher education are key institutions. They are not just about giving the luckiest chaps the jolliest time, as Chesterton once wrote of Oxford. From the economic point of view, they are a critical resource: the value added by human capital becomes more and more knowledge-based.[1]

The style of the PEVE provision is usefully captured by the DES's magazine *PICKUP in Progress: Updating Britain at Work.*

> Professional, Industrial and Commercial Updating (PICKUP) is a government programme covering England, Scotland and Wales. It helps colleges, polytechnics and universities to provide flexible, part-time education and training in the latest skills, knowledge and techniques for the employees of companies and organisations. . . .

The summer 1989 issue contains features on news, regional focus, innovations, coming events, and PICKUP contacts (the twelve PICKUP regional officers). It includes articles on 'The Changing Professions' and 'An Entrée for Colleges' dealing with training in the food-manufacturing industry. There is a piece on the use of video in the updating of American engineers ('I'm learning physics from Albert Einstein'), and on a Suffolk initiative with European links aimed at women returners. Part of an interview the national manager of PICKUP gave for the *Institution of Electrical Engineers Review* appears under the title '. . . True Professionals Will Wish to Take Responsibility for Their Own Updating . . .'

A further area of intended development in university adult education is mature entry to undergraduate programmes. Over the past two decades 10 per cent of the intake for undergraduate courses have been 21 or more years old. Both government and universities have been anxious to increase the percentage of older undergraduates for a range of reasons, from practical considerations such as compensating for the anticipated decline in demand for places by 18-year-olds (the fall in the birth-rate means that there will be 30 per cent fewer late teenagers in the 1990s) to more idealistic ambitions to make universities less middle-class in their student body. As one university typically noted in its 1989 plan, 'Entry to the University should be expanded as fast as relevant resources and facilities allow. Essential considerations involving the universities' responsibilities to the community are reinforced by national concerns about the low Age Participation Rate and speculation about the effect of the mid-1990s demographic decline.' The acknowledgement by virtually all universities and the government that the 1990s will be the decade of more mature students in undergraduate courses has made other developments favourable to adult students a priority for universities: these include credit transfer, modularisation of courses and greater awareness that discerning adults are more likely to be critical of poor teaching than are 18-year-olds.

As previously described, the universities are of great importance in the training of those who teach adults. The departments of adult education and other units which contribute to such work, ranging from short courses to PhDs, usually also promote research into the education of adults. In 1969 the Standing Conference on University Teaching and Research in the Education of Adults (SCUTREA) was founded 'to enable those in universities who engage in the teaching of and research into the teaching of adults to express and share their academic concerns'. SCUTREA has been important in the encouragement of training and research through such initiatives as its survey of universities in the mid-1970s which highlighted matters like the geographical gaps in course provision.

Unlike their counterparts in North America, English universities have been reluctant to provide part-time undergraduate degree courses. There have been honourable exceptions such as Birkbeck College within the University of London (the latter also previously notable for its external degree programme), or the pioneering work of the University of Hull

97

in the 1960s, but these were the exceptions. In 1969 the Open University transformed the situation, and one of the unfortunate results was a tendency of other universities to say that they did not need to offer part-time first degrees as that was now covered by the OU's provision. During the 1980s there was renewed interest in offering such courses, often following the Hull and Kent models of two stages, the first stage leading to the award of a certificate, and the second stage a degree. Cautious universities frequently began by allowing part-time degree adult students to attend the full-time day programmes. Separate evening provision was seen as too expensive in resources. As the supply of well-qualified 18-year-olds becomes less in the 1990s it can be expected that universities will be more sympathetic to the allocation of resources to separate part-time evening undergraduate courses.

The universities' contribution to part-time liberal adult education continues to be substantial with, including joint provision with the WEA, well over 300,000 enrolments in the United Kingdom (302,546 in 1986–87). With the decision of the DES to hand over its part-funding of such work to the Universities Funding Council (UFC) in 1989, the future may prove difficult. A UFC circular letter (15/89) of 10 July 1989 stated:

> At present there are three strands of funding: the FTE-based [part-time student numbers assessed as full-time equivalent students] grants for various types of CE paid as an indicated part of block grant; PICKUP and INSET grants; funding for extra-mural departments recently transferred from the DES and Welsh Office. From 1990/91 the separate funding of these strands will be replaced by an integrated arrangement based upon tenders submitted by universities for the delivery of a stated portfolio.

Although extra-mural work will be safeguarded during a transitional period, in the longer term the 1990s will see its increasing loss of subsidy and it will become provision for the affluent middle classes. When the UFC no longer earmarks such extra-mural allocations hard-pressed universities will use the money for other purposes. English universities do not have the same commitment to the citizens of their region as can be found in many American institutions.

Twenty-seven universities in England and Wales had 'responsible body' status prior to 1989 (i.e. they were allocated DES or Welsh Office money for the liberal education of adults). With over 600 full-time teaching and administrative staff and 8,000 part-time tutors the departments of adult education and extra-mural studies provided courses ranging from certificates in subjects such as archaeology to three-year tutorial classes in geology. Student motivations have always been diverse, but most are probably related to intellectual interest or professional and social roles. The programmes have pioneered many new developments in university provision such as the industrial day-release courses which began in the early 1920s, local history as a field of serious study, social-work training, and the use of computers with disadvantaged groups. The extra-mural class itself has been typified by a relaxed atmosphere, discussion as a large element, and an interaction between the scholarship of the tutor and the experience of life of the students. Where these characteristics have been brought to bear on specialist groups associated with extra-mural work, for example in courses for trade unionists, distinctive traditions have been established.

Good descriptions of these teaching methods are to be found in such books as Alan Rogers' *Teaching Adults* or Konrad Elsdon's earlier *Training for Adult Education*. Peter Jarvis's substantial contribution to the literature of adult education in recent years has added greatly to both these themes and related matters. Particularly useful are his *The Sociology of Adult and Continuing Education* and *Adult Learning in the Social Context*.[2]

The Workers' Educational Association

The WEA, as noted earlier, has some 900 branches and 1,500 affiliated organisatons. It is a voluntary body which is non-sectarian and non-party political. Its branches are organised into districts (Berks, Bucks and Oxon; Eastern; East Midlands; London; Northern; North Western; Southern; South Eastern; South Western; Western; West Lancs and Cheshire; West Mercia; Yorkshire North; and Yorkshire South. There are also Welsh, Scottish and Northern Ireland districts) each with a district office and responsible for appointing tutors to conduct the classes organised by the branches. The district looks after existing branches and aids in the creation of new ones. Students in the branches have considerable say in the running of the WEA, along with individual subscribers and representatives of affiliated organisations. An active branch will not only determine the subjects to be offered in the weekly class programme, but promote exhibitions, conferences, one-day schools, and raise issues of public concern. However, the 1918 WEA yearbook (*The WEA: Its Constitution and Activities*, p. 350) stated what continues to be the focus of its activities, 'The main work of the Association has been, and will continue to be, to arouse and satisfy the desire for education among adult men and women'.

Overseeing the work of a district is a council on which serve representatives of the branches, affiliated societies and individual subscribers. Each district has a full-time district secretary and field staff, whose number varies from district to district. A national conference meets biennially to agree policy, but each district has its own distinctive flavour. My experience of the West Lancs and Cheshire district over ten years, and then the East Midlands district over fifteen years, strongly confirms regional variations and the WEA's ability to encourage local volunteer and professional members' flair. Since its foundation in 1903 the WEA has had a remarkable ability to harness the enthusiasm of volunteers and, with a modest investment in full-time staff, has achieved substantial programmes of adult education. More difficult to assess, but without doubt of substantial importance to the well-being of English society, has been the WEA's creation of nuclei of caring citizens. In everything from working-class leadership to lobbies on environmental issues the WEA has raised the consciousness of the English. In typical English gloominess both the WEA and those outside have then spent the decades complaining that the association has not had full success in recruiting working-class men and women or that it has failed to influence sufficiently governments on educational matters. There is the fact of life in English educational innovation from the mechanics' institutes onwards that such initiatives tend to recruit the social class above that intended. And no educational institution ever has 100 per cent success in its objectives. The WEA on an annual national budget which would buy the jet engine in a single RAF Tornado enriches remarkably the life of some 200,000 citizens who attend its classes each year, and many more through less direct contact.

The Department of Education and Science recognises the WEA as a 'responsible body' for the provision of adult education and makes an annual grant. Since 1989 the DES has been discussing a system of local funding for the WEA districts by transferring resources to the local authorities through the revenue support grant mechanism. The WEA's national office would be funded directly by the DES. The other major source of outside funding comes from the local education authorities. Many districts have a close working relationship with their local university departments of adult education and extra-mural studies. The most notable example is the East Midlands district and its connection with the University of Nottingham, where some 60 per cent of the latter's extra-mural programme is in partnership with the WEA.

The 1973 Russell Committee (List of Recommendations 30) stated that

> The WEA should give particular attention to the following tasks: Education for the social and culturally deprived living in urban areas; Educational work in an industrial context; Political and social education; Courses of liberal and academic study below the level of university work.

The last of these was aimed at weakening its links with universities. Many in the association were unhappy about this proposal as they saw such traditions as the three-year tutorial classes as a central platform of their work, and highly

101

prized the WEA's links with the universities. The liberal adult education programmes had provided most of the volunteers who ran the branches and established the WEA's reputation as a provider of serious educational courses.

The Russell Report stated (sections 232–232.4):

In its evidence to us the WEA has pointed to four areas in which its recent experience shows possibilities of expansion that it would wish to pursue. In general terms these are all concerned with sectors of the population who might not otherwise be touched by adult education and they are therefore a logical development of the Association's traditional concern for the underprivileged. We strongly support the Association's desire to undertake such work. The four areas are: Education for the socially and culturally deprived living in urban areas. Many other bodies are engaged in such areas – local authorities through community development projects involving housing and social services departments as well as education, the Home Office, universities, and local organisations such as Councils of Social Service, community associations, neighbourhood committees and local action groups. The involvement of the WEA would have to be in a strictly educational role and closely integrated with the work of the other bodies. It would also have to be of an experimental and informal character, requiring new forms of activity and unfamiliar techniques. Work in an industrial context, especially classes held in factories or other workplaces, and programmes arranged in consultation with the TUC and with individual trade unions, including courses for shop stewards. Political and social education. Traditionally the WEA has believed that much of its work in general education was directed to greater social and political awareness as well as intellectual enlightenment. This conception we feel to have special value today. New avenues for activity have begun to appear in courses run in cooperation with OXFAM, SHELTER and similar socially oriented organisations, and in certain kinds of 'role educaton' for those engaged in local government and in social and political activity. Courses of liberal and academic study below the level of university work, intended either for those who find that this level and kind of course satisfies their intellectual ambition, or for those who wish to prepare for the more rigorous university courses. This is the area of provision where there is the greatest likelihood of overlapping with the work of the local education

authorities as academic studies come to find a place in the programmes of their centres. It is an area in which the role of
the WEA may gradually come to include a greater element of
promotional work, encouraging and supporting balanced programmes by local education authorities as well as making provision of its own.

The first three categories of work allocated by the Russell
Report to the WEA have been given the title within WEA
circles of 'Russell-type' provision. These contributions
expanded during the rest of the 1970s, often at the expense
of the liberal adult education programme. For example by
the end of the decade trade-union studies was up by 31 per
cent. Much of this was in partnership with the TUC education
department and local unions, and was mainly in the form of
day-release courses. After 1979 the rapid rise in unemployment saw a decline in such trade-union work, but a substantial increase in WEA initiatives directed at the unemployed.
Trade-union courses still represent the WEA's leading subject
group, although this is challenged by provision such as that
in history or in science (notably the field sciences).

Through the autonomy of its branches the WEA has been
more effective than its critics would give it credit for in
picking up and voicing a great number of contemporary English interests. Two areas of concern have come through
strongly to illustrate this. Firstly, the WEA now gives considerable attention to the women's movement which has
emerged in its ranks. Inequalities between the sexes are still
very apparent, but are now tolerated far less than by previous
generations. Despite the election of a female Prime Minister
there is a feeling that since 1979 women's rights have not
progressed, and in some areas have deteriorated. The WEA
has been good at providing a forum for debate and action on
such matters (as have other adult education institutions like
the National Institute of Adult Continuing Education and
the universities). Secondly, the WEA has effectively picked
up rural discontent and given expression to it. This has often
been stimulated by very practical considerations. For example
during the 1980s rural bus services became less comprehen-

sive. As WEA students found themselves unable to get a bus to their class in a nearby town or village, they raised such issues within the WEA.

In its recommendations to the secretary of the Reconstruction Committee dated 24 November 1916 (1918 WEA *Yearbook*, p. 349) the WEA proclaimed:

> That, since the character of British democracy ultimately depends on the collective wisdom of its adult members, no system of education can be complete that does not promote serious thought and discussion on the fundamental interests and problems of life and society, such as is promoted by the WEA. . . .

Like so much of the best of English adult education, the WEA has laboured hard to produce a better-educated citizenry. Democracy is always under threat, and Mansbridge and others were well aware of this.[3] The WEA has helped to equip the more vulnerable in English society to make their voice heard, and has provided one of the most effective platforms for the caring, articulate middle classes. At the same time these priorities have encouraged adult education classes and programmes full of quality and innovation.

Broadcasting

As such studies as Arthur Stock's *Adult Education in Great Britain* (NIACE, 1980) so ably confirmed, the institutions which have an impact on English adult education are legion. Equally, their contribution is often complex and difficult to set limits to. No area demonstrates this more clearly than broadcasting. The adult education impact of the BBC or the independent companies cannot be limited to the work of their formal educational broadcasts, or even to their contributions in areas like current affairs, natural history, science, the arts and drama.

In a paper given at a BBC dinner (Working Party for Educational Broadcasting) in Bath on 23 June 1988 the BBC's Director-General Michael Checkland pointed out that:

> Any organisation in society which is involved in the educational process, and this, of course, includes broadcasting – is inevitably

influenced by the changing scene and needs to respond to it, but also it has an impact of its own. In terms of skills, broadcasters can offer help, not only with the basic tools of literacy and numeracy, but with the growing demand for vocational training. The labour market is growing fast. The workplace is becoming more complex. We can offer retraining packages, such as basic training in subjects like computer competence, for which there seems an endless demand, and the topping up of professional skills, especially for teacher training and updating knowledge for social work. We are looking to use our unused transmitter time through the night on BBC 2 to provide a special service for the medical profession which wll be achieved by downloading material to video cassette recorders operated automatically by data pulses through the transmitter chain. More developments will follow. My second heading was 'knowledge', and television is unrivalled as a medium for increasing our knowledge, whether of the physical world, of our own recent history or of the culture, attitudes and experience of others. Because of this, there can be no hard or fast distinction between educational and general broadcasting. We, as public service broadcasters, have a responsibility to ensure that as rich and varied a range of output as possible is available to our national audiences. For our part in the UK, in a mixed terrestrial and satellite future, what is important is that education programmes continue to be made as part of the wide spectrum of programming of a public service broadcasting organisation and continue to be accessible to the whole nation and not just to any satellite-equipped minority. . . . Broadcasts are, or are seen as being, free, at the point of use, but in an age of the domestic video recorder, in the 1990s, the pressure may well be for the broadcasters to make and sell more educational media packages. In these circumstances what will be your stance? What will be the irreducible minimum of public educational needs which you feel should be met only by freely transmitted and openly available means of broadcasting? What, in the fields of health education, citizens' rights, access to basic education and the like, must at the very least continue to be available in this way? And what, conversely, perhaps in the field of professional training, business, hobbies and some recreational activities might need to be made available on a more commercial basis? One of the challenges of the next decade will be to get the correct balance between general availability and repackaged and specially focused and marketed material. . . .

My final heading was communication and understanding, the aim surely of all education! Understanding grows from knowledge and the ability to use that knowledge. No broadcasters with a commitment to education can fail to include a high percentage of informative and cultural programming in its general output, or fail to use its access to the general audience to sneak in a little overt education.

The Independent Broadcasting Authority (IBA) established a policy of 'workshops' where adult education policy for Independent Television (ITV) and Channel 4 was agreed for the following year. Each ITV company has a community and continuing education officer. There are regular liaison meetings with BBC staff. The free advance information pamphlet *TV Take-up* gives information on adult education provision.

Independent local radio has a membership of 35 stations in England with an educational output broadly based and covering topics such as health and parent education. There is increasing co-operation with local colleges and adult education centres. Social action broadcasting is of increasing importance.

The structure of BBC Education is usually similar to the commercial sector. BBC Education has five production departments (schools radio and television, continuing education radio and television, and the Open University production centre). A further department, educational broadcasting services, is responsible for the link between the users and the broadcasters and is formalised in the Educational Broadcasting Council. Two more recent developments have been the Educational Broadcasting Services Trust, to develop educational projects within and outside the BBC using non-licence-fee money, and this links with the Educational Developments Unit which, through the BBC's commercial arm, BBC Enterprises, creates new non-broadcast resources for sale.

BBC Education's output in 1988 was 1,396 hours for both television and radio, and 934 hours for the Open University. About £30 million is spent on education (including adult education) directly. The audiences for BBC Education's programmes can be huge, for instance those on healthy eating numbered 11 million, whilst the Sunday-evening broadcasts on spelling each had 6 million viewers. Where a narrower audience is targeted, such as 'See Hear' for the profoundly deaf and hard of hearing or 'Let's Go' for people with learning difficulties, then obviously the audience is much smaller.

In adult education the broadcasters have introduced much innovation in areas like the teaching of foreign languages and information technology. As already noted, broadcasting's impact on basic education has helped to make it a national issue and draw in the resources of other agencies through programmes such as 'On the Move', 'Write Now', 'Spelling It Out', and (from Yorkshire Television) 'Make It Count'.[4] Increasingly the broadcasters seek formal collaboration with other institutions involved in adult education (e.g. with the Royal Society of Arts on office skills, or the Business and Technician Education Council on 'Inside Science'). Series like 'In the Know', which looks at study skills and is broadcast on a Sunday evening, have helped to generate interest in further study with agencies such as the Open College.

Frequently the educational broadcasts have accompanying material such as books, pamphlets or cassettes. Those programmes produced for general output, but which can legitimately be seen as 'educational', such as David Attenborough's 'Life on Earth', have associated books which often become bestsellers. Magazines like *The Listener* also print material from selected broadcasts.

Broadcasters contribute massively to adult education from the specific, such as radio's programmes and packs on school-governor training, to the general cultivation afforded by a highly influential system which contains less mediocre output than that suffered by many other countries. As broadcasting is so accessible to the citizen the national debate about how to harness some of it to adult education needs to be vigorously pursued. In an age when greed is reputed to be king the 1988 Broadcasting White Paper did at least firmly accept the need for public-service broadcasting, which should reassure all those (since Lord Reith) mesmerised by broadcasting's educational mission.

Other adult education institutions

I have been selective in the organisations dealt with in this chapter, although I have tried to cover most of the major institutions in adult education. Nevertheless there are many other contributors to confirm that our society is permeated by consciously and unconsciously provided adult education. For example the churches are involved in extensive adult education programmes, both formal and informal. I did note, in a 1989 conference paper,

> From Adult Education's viewpoint it will probably be more fruitful to promote the 'religious needs' of the unchurched who make up a majority of the British population. Can Adult Education make a major contribution to the religious life of the community, and notably those who do not belong to a church?[5]

Nevertheless, religious bodies, both Christian and non-Christian, are substantial providers of adult education, as are the armed services, and various charitable organisations ranging from MIND (National Association for Mental Health) to the University of the Third Age. There are scores of agencies which there is neither space nor time to cover here, from the National Association for the Care and Resettlement of Offenders to Help the Aged. My apologies to readers and the important institutions concerned.

Notes

1 'Higher Education: the Next 25 Years' (DES, 1989).
2 A. Rogers, *Teaching Adults* (Open University Press, 1986); K. Elsdon, *Training for Adult Education* (Department of Adult Education, University of Nottingham, 1975); P. Jarvis, *The Sociology of Adult and Continuing Education* (Croom Helm, 1985) and *Adult Learning in the Social Context* (Croom Helm, 1987).
3 See B. Jennings, *Knowledge is Power: A Short History of the W.E.A. 1903–1978* (Department of Adult Education, University of Hull, 1979).
4 See H. A. Jones and A. H. Charnley, *Adult Literacy – A Study of its Impact* (NIACE, 1977).
5 M. D. Stephens, 'An Adult Educator Looks at Religious Education' in P. Jarvis (ed.) *New Directions in Adult Religious Edu-*

cation (Department of Educational Studies, University of Surrey, 1989).

Chapter 8

CONCLUSION: TRENDS, METHODS, FASHIONS AND PREJUDICES

A question or two

How can you do justice to adult education in a country with over 150,000 charities? England is amongst the most complex of societies and its adult education provision reflects this. There are broad trends and fashions at any point in time, but their local interpretation results in a multitude of forms. The programme at, say, Hatfield Polytechnic might be assumed to be the same as that at Middlesex Polytechnic, but it is not. A local education authority cookery class in Cumbria will have a tutor who produces a different curriculum to that offered under the same title in Cornwall. Training Agency courses may work to the same format, but the human factor enriches the result with various interpretations. Each meeting between a group of learners and a tutor is unique. As John Daines and Brian Graham noted of one aspect of this pluralism,

> individual adults do have different learning styles; in all probability they pass through a number of developmental stages and some aspects of their memory performance may change with age. Whatever the exact nature of the differences, there can be little doubt that compared with children, adults bring a massive amount of acquired knowledge and experience to any new learning situation. They also possess considerable practical experience of the process of acquiring new knowledge, opinions and skills, though little of this will have taken place in a classroom or with the help of a tutor. For many people 'learning through experience', whereby they solve problems, acquire skills and develop understanding and knowledge in their own manner, is likely to be the

preferred way of doing things. It follows that they are less likely to respond effectively to the formal teaching methods they endured at school.[1]

At any time there will be favoured forms of adult education, and less fashionable. Often government policy sets the fashions, although professional educationalists can be very influential. As we have seen the major allocation of resources at present, and in the foreseeable future, is to vocational adult education. As Sheila Innes wrote (paper made available to the author) two months after taking up her post as chief executive of the Open College,

> [The Open College] is employment-led. The UK has traditionally put a premium on 'knowing' rather than 'doing'. We have, as a nation, rewarded academic knowledge rather than vocational and personal competence. The new College is in business to make a distinctive, co-ordinated contribution to training and to the upgrading of skills in the workplace, using the strengths of both national and local television and radio, in addition to print, cassettes, computer software, kits and student services. The College will widen access to open learning primarily for those in employment, but also for those seeking jobs and wanting to acquire new and relevant skills. It will be a College for Everyone, open and accessible.

The key question has always been that posed by Sir Richard Livingstone in the bleak days of 1941: 'Why are we an uneducated nation and how can we become an educated one?'[2] Of course not everyone would agree that we are an uneducated nation. By the standards of a hundred years ago we are not, but the yardstick now is individual and international. What education does a citizen need to lead a full and satisfying life in our society? What education does a citizen enjoy in other countries? To take the latter question first, in 1989 Japan became the richest country on earth with assets at the end of 1987 of $43.7 trillion (as against the United States's $36.2 trillion). In an age where the British government rates economic performance as the most important consideration there is some justice in measuring ourselves by the Japanese yardstick. There is little doubt in the minds of the Japanese that educational investment is crucial to economic success. Japanese education has many limitations, of which the Japanese are increasingly aware, but Japanese citizens do have a higher level of education than their English counterparts. It is worth stressing once more that virtually all 18-year-olds are in full-time schooling, and well over a third go on to full-time university courses. Part-time higher education opportunities are more difficult to find, but an argument could be made that they are less necessary than in England. As Teruhisa Horio wrote in *Educational Thought and Ideology in Modern Japan*: 'In recent years education has increasingly come to be thought of as one of our most basic human rights, indeed the right by virtue of which all other modern rights ultimately derive their substance and meaning'.[3] Teruhisa later notes

> If the People's right to learn is inconceivable apart from the idea of popular sovereignty, then popular sovereignty is unthinkable apart from the right to learn. In fact, as soon as one begins to think of education as the activity which protects the vitality of popular sovereignty, it should become abundantly clear that the right to learn must be guaranteed so that the People can autonomously achieve full consciousness of their status as rulers of our democratic society. Hence the right to an education must be included among the rights of citizens in a popularly controlled society because it cultivates the sensibilities necessary for upholding a free form of political life. (pp. 383–4).

It may surprise us that the Japanese, having developed an education system to serve the economy, should now be so interested in the broader issues of citizenship. This was an English obsession in the earlier part of the century during the development of the Workers' Educational Association, local education authorities' non-vocational adult education classes, and the creation of university extra-mural departments. The Japanese have discovered the need to promote both vocational education and that broader-based provision which seems to produce what Harold Wiltshire tellingly dubbed 'reflective citizens'. The Japanese would appear to be trying to avoid the English malady of either/or-ism. With our reluctance to put money into education we are unlikely to equip anyone other than the prosperous middle classes to face effectively a society of ever-greater complication.

Educational guidance

With relatively limited resources going into all forms of English education the dissemination of better information on what is provided has been one of the most important developments within adult education during recent years. There are now a number of databases to guide the would-be consumer through the maze of provision which has grown up over the decades. Many have been set up with government aid and encouragement. MARIS-NET, based at Ely, is a national on-line information service on industrial and commercial short courses and self-study resources. NERIS (National Educational Resources Information Service) at Woburn is a database dealing with learning materials and their availability. EMIE (Educational Management Information Exchange) at Slough deals in information on educational policy and practice such as abstracts of local education authority documentation. PRESTEL EDUCATION at Telephone House in London collates training and education information and has a telesoftware service. The National Institute of Adult Continuing Education has three databases, the ACE-Database of research and resource material in adult continuing education; ABE-Database of resource materals for tutors/volunteers; and REPLAN Database of research and resource materials on adult education and unemployment. AIMER (Access to Information on Multicultural Educational resources) at Bulmershe College of Higher Education has details of multicultural ephemera and materials not available commercially. BARD-SOFT-Database on software for special needs at Newcastle-upon-Tyne Polytechnic is Europe's largest such database. The British Library Bibliographic Services Division has an on-line automated service called BLAISE-LINE.

For many adult educators amongst the best known of the databases is ECCTIS (Educational Counselling and Credit

Transfer Information Service) at Milton Keynes. John Taylor, ECCTIS's liaison manager, was formerly secretary of the Advisory Council for Adult and Continuing Education during its six years of life. ECCTIS has been funded by the Department of Education and Science which has put in some £4 million to provide a national information service based on a computerised database of higher and further education courses. At present ECCTIS has information on 60,000 such courses in more than 700 institutions. It also collects information on non-standard entry requirements and credit transfer schemes. The aim is to provide a central source of information for would-be students, those involved in educational counselling and careers guidance, and employers.

ECCTIS was founded in 1983 with a three-year pilot scheme. A further three-year contract covered 1986–88. From January 1990 a five-year contract to run ECCTIS has been awarded to a consortium of The Times Network Services Ltd, Hobsons Publishing Ltd, the Polytechnics Central Admissions Service, British Telecom, and the Careers Research and Advisory Centre. Over the five years it is expected that the DES's subvention will be phased out, although it will still take responsibility for quality and future development.

The database holds information on course location, content, level, mode, duration, qualification received and entry requirements. It is accessible on-line through PRESTEL, CAMPUS 2000, and the Training Agency's TAPs scheme. Information is also available on compact disc, and by post or telephone enquiry to ECCTIS itself. In 1988 ECCTIS responded to over 140,000 on-line searches, with August the peak month with almost 70,000 stimulated by those seeking information on course vacancies.

The consortium which now runs ECCTIS illustrates the fast development and diversity of the field. The Times Network Services (TTNS) is part of News International plc and since 1984 has provided electronic communication and information services within education. British Telecom's PRESTEL and TTNS in 1989 integrated their services to form CAMPUS 2000. Hobsons Publishing issues a number of education and careers directories. The Polytechnics Central Admissions Service is a charitable status company, as is the Careers Research and Advisory Centre, which has been in education and careers guidance since 1964.

Of the 59,532 course totals on the ECCTIS database in December 1988 non-advanced further education provided the greatest number, with 32,090. First-degree courses were listed as 12,741, taught postgraduate courses 6,725 and advanced further education courses numbered 7,976. Of the enquiries 60 per cent were about first degrees, whilst advanced and non-advanced further education each accounted for 15 per cent and the remaining 10 per cent was for information on postgraduate courses. Part-time study enquiries rose from 8 per cent in 1987 to 17 per cent in 1988. As the ECCTIS information sheet for Winter 1988–89 notes, 'This significant shift suggests that, within the substantially increased number of on-line enquiries handled, relatively more are coming from adults than from school-leavers'.

ECCTIS Facts 7 sheet (Spring 1989) is devoted to credit transfer schemes and illustrates well how the creation of specially focused agencies can give momentum to developments. Credit transfer is defined as: alternatives to the conventional school-leaving qualifications required for initial entry to higher education; entry with exemption from some part of the course because of higher qualifications or experience; entry to shortened courses designed specifically for those with prior qualifications or experience; transfer, on successful completion of part or all of a course, to a higher-level course. Obviously such considerations can have particular relevance to adults. Within the listing there is reference to 'experience' and there is increasing interest in experiential learning. Can a person's experience be counted as equivalent to coursework? Adult education will have to develop systems of such equivalency. Some of the most interesting work in this area has been done by Norman Evans.[4]

Educational guidance for adults is obviously going to be a key feature in the coming decades. The National Association of Educational Guidance Services (NAEGS) has given greater shape to the many initiatives, often of a local nature, since such developments became more common in the 1970s. The association has proclaimed eight principles: educational guidance to adults is the primary purpose of the service; it is impartial and client-centred; it promotes equality of opportunity for learning; it is independent of the interests of any supporting agency or institution; it is readily accessible to all adult clients; it makes available information on the whole range of continuing education; it incorporates a network of educational providers, information services and related agencies; and it is free of charge to the general public. NAEGS's north-eastern membership, taking an example of one region, includes Barnsley Adult Educational Guidance and Information Service, Bradford Education Advice Service for Adults, Halifax's Education Shop, Hull Educational Guidance Service for Adults, Humberside Educational Guidance Service for Adults, Leeds Educational Guidance Service, Newcastle-upon-Tyne Linked Educational Advisory Service for Adults, Rotherham Educational Guidance Centre for Adults, Sheffield Adult Guidance and Information Service, South Tyneside and Wearside Linked Educational Advisory Service for Adults, and Wakefield Educational Counselling and Guidance for Adults.

Educational guidance, ever since the Advisory Council for Adult and Continuing Education's report *Links to Learning* (1979), is seen as a two-stage process in adult education. Not only is it to help students find programme places where there are relevant vacancies, but adults are to be helped towards learning. Writing of educational guidance and its future in adult education, John Taylor noted:

Student dissatisfaction and drop-out rates are measures of the lack of guidance for those who have actually got into the system. Most adults have never got that far. Widely available and well publicised guidance facilities could help change that and transform need into demand. . . . Greater professionalism is going to be important; that means appropriate staff training and perhaps professional qualifications. More computerisation is inevitable. More guidance staff are needed for the front line work, backed by computer-based information tools. The same demographic shift which is now boosting continuing education, will in turn boost the need for guiding adults into the newly expanding provision. All of this depends on a corresponding increase in the amount of research and development.[5]

A training programme suggested by Ray Woolfe, Stephen Murgatroyd and Sylvia Rhys is something of a commentary on what is good adult education. They propose what they call agenda items for training helpers of adults:

> Understanding adult life as a process of development and change and the implications of this for the provision of formal curricula and the enhancement generally of a wide range of learning opportunities for adults outside formal institutions; understanding the motivation behind and the nature of adult learning, particularly its emotional base; understanding the influences of social, cultural and economic factors upon the willingness of adults to learn and the direction of this learning; an awareness of the need to develop bridges beween the worlds of education and work and personal private lives; a knowledge of how to work within systems so as to promote organizational change; an understanding of the complexity of interpersonal relationships and of the important part which qualities such as empathy, warmth and genuineness play in such relationships; some expertise in basic counselling skills such as active, attending listening, asking open-ended questions and encouraging specificity and concreteness; a recognition of the open-ended nature of the helping process and the need for the helper to carry on learning in order to practise it more competently; a recognition of the role of the self in relationships and an acceptance of responsibility for personal development by the person seeking help.[6]

Those with pressures on their available resources may view such a list as too demanding, although a careful application of the points made will prove more effective and less costly in the medium to long term. Adult education and training will always be justified in investment terms as providing more productive workers or because of the personal benefit it brings to a student. As already suggested, government resources will continue to go towards the former, whilst an increasingly affluent middle class will be expected to pay the economic cost, however that is estimated, for adult education for personal enrichment. This leaves endless grey areas and questions. What about education for the adult's role in society? It may come within the second category, but be at least as important to the well-being of the community as updating or retraining for work. For example we suffer greatly in environmental terms because farmers have had much adult education provision to improve their yields per acre, but little on their role in society. Their enhanced incomes and productivity leave the rest of the community to cope with such environmental consequences as soil erosion, excessive nitrates in drinking water, and a denuded bird and animal life. In the future, in this instance it will be much more important to educate farmers in their obligations to fellow citizens than to update further their knowledge of high-yield farming. Too much vocational adult education is focused narrowly on favoured aspects of a single industry. It is as if the modern soldier was taught only the job of killing his enemy. This is only one role, and often the least important, of a multitude for which the soldier of the late twentieth century has to be prepared.[7]

Polytechnics

The trends, methods, fashions and prejudices within English adult education are much in evidence in the contribution of polytechnics, which have frequently been more willing to innovate than longer-established institutions like universities. During discussions with the Polytechnic of Central London in the late 1970s, I recall our surprise at its greater involvement of academic staff in all forms of adult education than we had achieved at Nottingham. Ideas over short-course provision in both vocational and non-vocational adult education and approaches to funding which have since become more commonplace were already well established. Particularly in the governmental drive for more updating provision in higher education the polytechnics have had great importance, but they have also been quicker to establish a broad range of part-time first degrees and access courses, and to experiment with fresh delivery systems for familiar styles of programme such as liberal adult education with lunchtime lectures and experiments in distance education. It is significant that of the full-time students in England's 29 polytechnics, less than 50 per cent enter directly from school. Polytechnics have a high percentage of mature students who have been attracted by flexible admission requirements, modular courses, and a generally more welcoming atmosphere than that found in most universities.

The 1966 government White Paper, *A Plan for Polytechnics and Other Colleges*, aimed at a broader-based higher education, and the polytechnics' contribution to adult education has gone a long way to justify this ambition. Their short-courses programmes now recruit over 90,000 students each year, and they have helped to break down higher education prejudices over types of teaching, many subject areas, and some audiences. In part-response other institutions in higher education have shown more adventurousness in their approaches to adult students. Polytechnics may not be quite as fashionable amongst the ever-class-driven English as universities, but their more flexible view of what makes a good contribution to a rapidly changing society has been of considerable importance. In the main they have been more imaginative and open-minded than either the universities or government, and this has benefited adult education. Universities and governments have been conservative (after all, even the so-called radical Thatcher administration has looked back to a nineteenth-century model). Polytechnics have been hungrier and more likely to be sensitive to society and its trends.

In 1981 the Polytechnic Association for Continuing Education was founded. The aim was to promote collaboration between polytechnics within adult education. Those colleges of higher education with an interest in continuing education can become associate members. As with similar associations, it provides an annual conference and various workshops. The creation of such an organisation signals the coming of age of the polytechnics in adult education.

The NIACE's policy discussion paper 'Adults in Higher Education' (1989) includes in its recommendations many of the themes and initiatives found in the present book:

Increased funds will be needed for access and other preparatory courses, effectively to foster higher participation rates amongst adults in higher education (1.4); opportunities for employees to gain high level skills and training in higher education should be widened through a universal scheme of paid education leave (1.5); professional bodies should review current policies on entry and validaton in collaboration with providers of higher education, to ensure that adult students in higher education are not precluded from entry to the professions (1.6); institutions of higher education should have a clear statement on access addressed (amongst other things) to: recruitment policy, needs analysis and outreach, publicity, selection procedures, prior qualifications and experience, access routes, collaborative systems, physical access, student support, and financial support (1.7); institutions should have clear policies on guidance, covering such matters as: networking with other guidance agencies; mechanisms for initial contact; feedback mechanisms; internal guidance (1.8); institutions should review their curricula from the point of view of adult students, to reflect their ability to be self-directed. In particular, there should be more opportunities for students over 21 to negotiate their own programmes of study, through the use of learning contracts (1.9); more open learning should be employed, wherever adult students are present in significant numbers. Curricula should be built more around students' experience (1.10); in general, full-time courses should be available on a part-time basis. Institutions might consider allowing part-time students who are in employment to negotiate a programme of action-based learning, around their work experience; normally, for part-time courses, there should be some short periods of optional full-time study, preferably on a residential basis (1.11); self-assessment and peer-group assessment might be used more, alongside more conventional modes of assessment; assessment might also include accreditation of work-based learning on employers' premises (1.12); institutions should review their programmes of study to see how far they can be offered on a modular, credit-point basis. Programmes could be designed jointly with industry, allowing students to gain credit for their work-based learning (1.13); institutions will need to develop a focused staff development programme, to assist teaching staff in their different roles in interacting with mature students, e.g. admissions, guidance, course design, use of information technology, and teaching strategies. The needs of non-teaching staff should be taken into account (1.17).

Of course, many institutions, whether in higher education or elsewhere, can already justly claim that these recommendations have been implemented before this discussion paper was published, but many who teach in universities, polytechnics and colleges of higher education have been less sensitive to the needs of adult students than some other sectors of education. Not long ago a distinguished professor of chemistry told me that he was against the training of university staff as it was important that undergraduates were badly taught so that they had to strive harder to compensate. The same man also admitted that he was mainly interested in research, and therefore concentrated on those undergraduates who would get first-class honours and go on to a PhD programme. Such a colleague may be one of a dying breed, but I doubt it. Most academics are first attracted into a university career by the chance to pursue their intellectual interests and, understandably, that remains their first love.

Extra resources can persuade most educationalists to give some of their time. In non-vocational adult education and some areas of vocational adult education strong ideals are often held and the allocation of further money may not be the only factor to produce further initiatives. However, with the Training Agency's massive contribution to adult education the culture of much of the field has changed. For example there are now 4,000 managing agents, including many private companies, on the Training Agency's payroll contracted to provide training for a million young people and unemployed adults. In 1989 the National Audit Office's report, *Department of Employment: Provision of Training Through Managing Agents*, expressed some unease over the Training Agency becoming many agents' major source of income. It was suggested that some 6 per cent of the approved training organisations failed to maintain the required standards, and that financial controls were frequently too loose. Where contracted places were unfilled (e.g. 109,000 YTS places in 1987–88) there were few attempts to recover fees. Such a system might be expected to produce a managing agent with a somewhat different outlook to, say, the LEA community college adult educator. There is a need to accommodate and cherish both.

The future

Although there has been little government interest in such formal legislation as paid educational leave (International Labour Organisation Convention 140 of 1974, 'leave granted to a worker for educational purposes for a specified period during working hours, with adequate financial entitlements'), which France has had since the 1970s, there is, as we have seen, increasing sympathy in official and industrial circles to the further and substantial development of vocational adult education. This is the most obvious area where there will be a greater allocation of national resources. The British economy continues to perform less well than that of such trading rivals as Japan and West Germany and an obvious difference between the United Kingdom and such states is a less well-educated and trained population. As J. E. Thomas has written of Japan:

> Societies can only be properly understood through a study of their history. Education, and in particular the education of adults, can only be understood through an awareness of the structure of society, and the historical processes by which that structure has been shaped. The process of adult education is powerful because it consummates experience and knowledge. In short, exposure of adults to education, to ideas which are consonant with the totality of their experience, is a major source of social change and development.... There are not many major societies in which the consciousness of history and tradition are stronger than in Japan. Nor are there many societies in which such high expectations have been placed upon adult education to integrate the

most desirable features of that tradition, and to eliminate the worst.[8]

Little in the history of England has enouraged the placing of a high value on education and training, in contrast to Buddhism and many of the Chinese traditions passed on to Japan. Somehow the Christian tradition, whilst providing much education, failed to establish in England a prized position for education. In the past relative government indifference and allocation of resources has confirmed education and training as lacking in prestige. Belated and determined efforts, although sometimes misdirected, are now being put into vocational adult education.

Non-vocational adult education faces an increasing demand from the general public in England, but is less favoured than in the past in the allocation of State and local government resources. The future will see the continuation of this trend, resulting in such provision being for the relatively affluent. If the demand for non-vocational adult education courses still grows then, as in Japan, private provision with high fees will be part of the developing adult education picture.

The current approach to teaching in vocational adult education is based on that developed since the last century in liberal adult education. The Further Education Unit's *Newsletter* for Spring 1989 stated,

> As the variety of learners in FE increases, there is a need to find ways of customising and individually tailoring educational provision to suit each student's personal requirements. Work will focus specifically on: open/flexible learning methods; the curriculum of guidance; modularisation; the application of curriculum frameworks.

This confirms that the unfortunate approaches to industrial and commercial education which emerged from the Skinnerian beliefs of the 1960s are now less in fashion.

In the 1919 Report (Sections 223 and 224) the adult-student-centred approach was firmly established:

> The teacher of adult classes undertakes work which, while it varies according to the kind of class and nature of the subject, is,

if properly performed, not less exacting than that of an intra-mural teacher in a university. He encounters critical audiences. He must be able not merely to lecture, but to answer questions, to meet difficulties, and to hold his own in discussion. He may exercise a great influence, but only if he never attempts to rely on authority. He has frequently to expose his knowledge, such as it is – and also, if he is wise, his ignorance – and to encourage the students, who are colleagues, rather than pupils, to pass their own judgements upon them. Such work cannot be done success-fully except by men and women who have a wide intellectual background. But intellectual qualifications are not the only point which needs to be considered in the selection of a teacher of adult classes. Equally important are qualities which cannot be discovered merely by an examination of academic records. Unlike most intra-mural teachers, the teacher of adult classes is con-cerned with students who have considerable practical experience, have formed their convictions upon the basis of it and who are often more mature in mind than himself ... he must be ready not merely to do the formal work of education involved in teaching a class, but also to give time and energy to promoting a temper of comradeship and mutual helpfulness amongst its members. . . .

The twin traditions of non-vocational and vocational adult education have come together in the style of teaching now favoured. The future for both is one of expansion, but with almost all State resources being directed to vocational adult education. As so often in the past, those who have had an above-average amount of education already will be the ones who can afford to pay increasingly high fees for non-vocational classes. When it comes to most forms of adult education the middle classes usually come off best. The question for the future in England is still the unanswered one of how to achieve a learning society.

Notes

1 J. Daines and B. Graham, *Adult Learning. Adult Teaching* (Department of Adult Education, University of Nottingham, 1988), p. 1.
2 R. Livingstone, *The Future in Education* (Cambridge University Press, 1941), p. 1.

3 H. Teruhisa, *Educational Thought and Ideology in Modern Japan* (University of Tokyo Press, 1988), p. 3.

4 See, for example, N. Evans, *Post Education Society: Recognising Adults as Learners* (Croom Helm, 1984).

5 J. Taylor, 'Educational Guidance for Adults in the UK: Developments through the 1980s' in M. Zukas (ed.) *Papers from the Transatlantic Dialogue: SCUTREA/AERC/CASAE* (School of Continuing Education, University of Leeds, 1988), pp. 429–30.

6 R. Woolfe, S. Murgatroyd and S. Rhys, *Guidance and Counselling in Adult and Continuing Education* (Open University Press, 1987), pp. 186–7.

7. For example, see M. D. Stephens (ed.) *The Educating of Armies* (Macmillan, 1989).

8 J. E. Thomas, *Learning Democracy in Japan* (Sage, 1985), p. 2.

INDEX

Access Centres 55
Access courses 65, 66, 67, 68, 69, 73–4, 83, 105–6, 119, 120
Access to Learning for Adults 66–9
accommodation 35, 38, 83–4, 88
Adult Literacy and Basic Skills Unit 4, 89–90, 93
adult schools 33
Advisory Council for Adult and Continuing Education 114, 116
Advisory Council for the Supply and Training of Teachers 38–9
Agricultural Training Board 40
Alston Hall College 86
andragogy 5
antiquarian societies 25
apprenticeships 55
Arkwright, Richard 19
Armed Forces 44, 108, 118
art galleries 24–5
Ashby Report (1953) 36–7
Association of British Correspondence Colleges 45–6
Attenborough, David 107

B & Q 77
Baker, Kenneth 90
balancing studies 3
Barnes, Neil ix
Barnet College of Further Education 63
Basic Skills Accreditation Initiative 90
Bates, Tony 61–2
Batley 31
Bayley, R. S. 20–1
Benson, Ian ix
Bird, M. 94
Birkbeck College 97
Birmingham 27
Birmingham University 27
Board of Education 30, 32, 35

Brighouse, Tim 8
British Association of Settlements 88
British Institute of Adult Education 34, 35
British Library 113
British Museum 25
British Petroleum 49
British Telecom 57, 114
broadcasting 39, 44, 61, 62, 65, 70, 72, 74, 104–7, 111
Broadcasting White Paper (1988) 107
Brougham, Henry 20
Bulmershe College of Higher Education 113
Burne-Jones, Edward 21
Business & Technician Education Council 44, 67, 107

Callaghan, James 2
Cambridge University 27, 28, 95
Cambridgeshire 36, 84
Camden 66
Canine Studies Institute 46
Canterbury 25
Careers Research and Advisory Centre 114–5
Careers Service 69
Carnegie Trust 32
Central and West London Open College 67
Certificate in Open Learning Delivery 78
Charnley, Alan 94
Chartists 21
Checkland, Michael 104–6
Chesterton, G. K. 96
Chorley 23, 86
Christian Association for Adult Continuing Education 46
Christian Socialists 21
churches 46, 108

Index

Educational Counselling and Credit
    Transfer Information
    Service 57, 113–5
educational settlements 33–4
Elsdon, Konrad 10, 99
Employment & Training Act
    (1973) 40
Employment for the 1990s 49
Employment Training
    initiative 51–2, 56
English for speakers of other
    languages 89–90
Enterprise in Higher Education
    initiative 59
environmental issues 118
ethnic minorities 52, 73, 88, 93,
    113
Eton 21
European Bureau of Adult
    Education 94
European Economic
    Community 50, 55
Evans, Norman 115
evening classes 21, 22, 29
evening institutes 34, 37–8
examinations 45–6, 55, 63
experiential learning 115

female education and
    training 27–8, 31, 33, 43, 47,
    55, 67, 73, 84, 93, 96, 103
female employment 5
Field Studies Council 46, 93
Fircroft College 33–4
FlexiStudy 63–4
Floodlight 84
foreign study tours 33
Fowler, Norman 90
Fox, Samuel 16
France 122
Freeman, Richard 63
full-time staff 38, 86, 88, 89, 91, 99,
    100
Further Education Unit 10, 80–1,
    123
*Future Development of Open
    Learning, The* 79

Gateway courses 63

Germany 17, 24, 27, 44–5, 57, 77,
    122
Giamatti, Bartlett 10
Glasgow 32
Glasgow University 27
government leadership 44–5, 48,
    49–50
Graham, Brian 110–1
Gray, Asa 27
Great Debate 2
Green, Michael 43
Griffith, Colin 85
Gwent College of Higher
    Education 37

Hackney 66
Hackney Adult Education
    Institute 69
Hackney College 69
Hackney Education Advice
    Service 69
Hall, Dorothea 79
Handy, Charles 7
Hardy, David ix, 56–7
Hatfield Polytechnic 110
health and safety 53
Health and Safety Acts 58
health education 65, 106
*High Technology National
    Training* 60
Higham Hall 86
Home Office 91, 102
Hooper, Baroness 82
Horncastle Residential College 86
Horsbrugh, Florence 36
Hotel and Catering Industry
    Training Board 40
Hudson, J. W. 17–18
Hughes, Thomas 21
Hull University 97–8

ICI 77
*Improving Quality in Further
    Education* 60
industrial and vocational adult
    education 3, 5, 40, 43–5,
    49–60, 75–9, 95, 102, 111, 123–4
industrial revolution 1, 14, 17, 19,
    77

128

Index

Maurice, Frederick Denison 21
mechanics' institutes 17–19, 22,
    23, 24, 25, 101
Methodism 16–17
Middlesex Polytechnic 110
Midwinter, Eric ix, 5
Miller, John 60
miners 15–16
Ministry of Education 36
Ministry of Reconstruction 12
mobility 6
Montefiore Community Education
    Centre 69
Morpeth, Ros ix, 64–5
Morris, Henry 35–6
Murgatroyd, Stephen 117
museums 17, 24–6
Museums Act (1845) 25
mutual improvement 20

Napoleon 17
National Council for Educational
    Technology 79–80
National Council for Vocational
    Qualifications 10–12, 51,
    58–9, 78, 92
National Council for Voluntary
    Organisations 46
National Extension College 61–5
National Federation of Community
    Organisations 46
National Federation of Voluntary
    Literacy Schemes 47
National Gallery 25
National Institute of Adult
    Continuing Education 34, 80,
    82, 89, 90, 92–4, 103, 113, 120–1
National Open College
    Network 67–9
National Training Task Force 50,
    53
National Union of Railwaymen 32
Neolithic revolution 14
New Job Training Scheme 55
New Training Initiative, A 54
*New Training Initiative, A: An
    Agenda for Action* 54–5
Newcastle Commission (1861) 22
Newcastle Polytechnic 113

1919 Report 12, 47, 123–4
Nonconformists 16–17
non-formal learning 6
non-vocational adult
    education 8–10, 21
North America 8
North London College 69
North of England Council for
    Promoting the Higher Education
    of Women 28
Nottingham 28
Nottingham Adult School 16
Nottingham University 28–9, 38,
    95, 101, 118
Nottinghamshire County
    Council 87–8

older students 47, 52
    see also mature students
Open Business School 72
Open College 43–5, 75–9, 83, 107
Open College Federation of the
    North West 67–8
Open College of South London 67
open learning 61–81, 83, 90, 92,
    111, 120, 123
Open Learning Business, The 60
Open Tech 55
Open University 36, 39, 43, 61,
    62–3, 65, 69–75, 98, 106
*Open University into the 1990s,
    The* 73–4
Oxford University 27, 28, 30, 31,
    96
Oxfordshire 35

paid educational leave 93, 120, 122
Paine, Nigel 61
parent education 106
part-time degrees 37, 97–8, 119
part-time organisers 38
part-time teachers 29, 32, 38, 39,
    86, 88, 89, 91, 99
payment-by-results 23
Pedder, Sue ix, 67–8
Peers, Robert 12–13, 29
Penny Magazine 20
Penzance Natural History and
    Antiquarian Society 25